The Child Catcher

The Child Catcher

A Fight for Justice and Truth

ANDREW BRIDGE

A REGALO PRESS BOOK
ISBN: 979-8-88845-042-0
ISBN (eBook): 979-8-88845-043-7

Cover Design by Conroy Accord

Publishing Team:
Founder and Publisher – Gretchen Young
Editorial Assistant – Caitlyn Limbaugh
Managing Editor – Madeline Sturgeon
Production Manager – Alana Mills
Production Editor – Rachel Hoge
Associate Production Manager – Kate Harris

All people, locations, events, and situations are portrayed to the best of the author's memory. While all of the events described are true, many names and identifying details have been changed to protect the privacy of the people involved.

As part of the mission of Regalo Press, a donation is being made to Court-Appointed Special Advocates (CASA), a national volunteer organization for foster children, as chosen by the author.

New York • Nashville
regalopress.com

Published in the United States of America
2 3 4 5 6 7 8 9 10

To the families of David Dolihite and Eddie Weidinger, and to the Survivors of The Eufaula Adolescent Center and MacLaren Hall.

"Children, where are you? I know you're here somewhere. I've lots of lovely goodies for you.... And all free today.... Come along my little dears, my little mice. Come to me. What will it be? Ice cream? Strawberry, chocolate, vanilla. It's all inside. Come along, my little dears. Come on. Come inside. Not a penny to pay. Yes, come on. Get in. Go inside, my little dears!"

—Roald Dahl, *The Child Catcher*

"In the use of power the best of men can rarely be trusted."

—Dr. Peter Bryce, founder of the Alabama Insane Hospital

"We were told Eufaula had a swimming pool, horses, basketball, a football field... everything a teenager would love."

—David Dolihite's father

The following story is true. The events described are based on oral histories; interviews with children and adults; court testimony, expert evaluations, and depositions; briefs and other documents filed with the court; along with the court's findings and rulings. Biographies, newspaper accounts, and independent research have also been relied upon. Out of respect for the privacy of individuals, some names and identifying details have been changed. See the source notes in the back for additional information.

Introduction

I wrote *Hope's Boy* sixteen years ago. In that memoir, I shared my life with my mom, Hope. I wrote about our lives together while she developed paranoid schizophrenia and apart while I grew up in foster care. I was six when Los Angeles County took me from her and decided to place me in MacLaren Hall. Located on the county's arid outskirts, MacLaren had been an abandoned polio hospital before it was turned into a holding facility for foster children. The facility's maze of wards, corridors, and basements could house more than three hundred children, from day-old infants to eighteen-year-olds. The population quickly swelled into a confused mix of foster children and older adolescents transferred from packed juvenile detention halls and camps. The result was a chaotic and violent compound. Despite repeated calls from grand juries, investigative reporting, and the public to shut the facility down—even outright demolish it—Los Angeles County defended MacLaren and kept it running. I was there for one year, and what happened has never left me.

After graduating from Harvard Law School, my career advocating for children's rights began at another state facility, one that was part of the sweeping, decades-long civil rights lawsuit *Wyatt v. Stickney*. The federal class action covered the thousands of individuals who had been sent to Alabama's psychiatric institutions, regardless of age, gender, mental illness, or even the lack of one. At the time, I was new to practicing law—the most time I had spent in a courtroom was as a boy growing up in foster care. My role was to represent the children at Alabama's largest facility for children, located in the rural southeast corner of the state.

The Eufaula Adolescent Center held 120 children, and Alabama began operating it around the same time I was leaving MacLaren Hall. Many children there were in foster care or about to enter it, and nearly all came from homes with hardened backgrounds like mine. Eufaula had a long and well-known history of violence, including abuse by staff and other children. It also had a history of covering up that violence. Like MacLaren, Eufaula was the place Alabama refused to surrender. What became a lifetime of defending children's rights began by returning to what I remembered from my first day without my mom—my first year in the system spent at MacLaren.

Facilities like MacLaren and Eufaula continue to operate across the country. Many are owned by for-profit corporations that advertise themselves as private residential treatment programs for "troubled teens" but remain largely exempt from regulation and oversight. State and local authorities run others for children in foster care, juvenile justice, and mental health systems. Certainly not all of them, but too many remain the subjects of investigations based on reports of harm done to children. I have sat with children confined to them and listened to their stories. They tell me about their parents and friends, neighborhoods and schools—about a time when their lives were different. They talk about finding their way back to the things they remember. Their forgiveness is extraordinary. They are the bravest children I have ever known.

I have written this book for the thousands of children in those places. This is the story of what brought me to an isolated institution in rural Alabama and my fight for the children of Eufaula. Before I went to Eufaula, I did everything I could to forget being a boy who had been put in another institution. I pushed and pulled until I had the education and honors that I needed. I did what I could to erase my past and replace it with an ordinary life. Part of me never wanted to go to Eufaula, but I went anyway.

Chapter One

One night in early March 1992, the older boys were crowded in the TV room when a shoving match erupted in the ward. Nothing that couldn't be handled right there, except for David. He was already in the seclusion room when the charge nurse called for more than the usual two men. It was shortly after nine o'clock, and Eufaula's grounds were as dark and quiet as the thickets of piney woods outside its barbed-wire fences. The institution's central administrative building had been closed for hours. The senior employees who wore suits and crisp dresses had left for the evening. Yet within minutes of the nurse's call, the darkened lawns were covered with a knot of orderlies, security guards, and groundskeepers.

A wiry fifteen-year-old with the body of a child, David was considered a "problem" from the get-go. A lonely boy, now with flashes of a temper, he ached for fishing trips and his father's pickup, his mother's complaints that he slept in too late on Saturdays, the walk he took alone to school. He missed the things that hadn't mattered before.

Jeff McCowell told the assembled group of men where they were headed. The facility's night director, McCowell didn't have to say much. Everyone there had done it before. A few of the men bickered, complaining it was close to the end of their shift or the start of a break, but work at the children's mental institution was good, the wage enough to support a family in one of Alabama's poorest counties. Those jobs weren't easy to get, and when a man found one, he kept it. That's why McCowell didn't need to press. He waited for the men to finish their grousing, then led them down the slick, glassy lawns.

Pacing ahead through the dark, McCowell tugged open the rusted metal door to the boys' ward and headed up to the third floor. Teenagers gawked from their bedroom doors, stripped to their T-shirts and underwear for bed. McCowell cut to the front and peered through the observation slat of the seclusion room. Drunk with a fresh shot of Thorazine, David lay against the cinder-block wall. His bare flat chest slumped to his belly. His socked feet spread from the new pair of jeans his mother had packed the night he left. The charge nurse inched away when McCowell stepped to her station and held out his palm for the key. Returning to the strip of scratched glass, he stabbed the key into the lock and shouldered open the seclusion door.

David did nothing.

McCowell stepped closer and bent to the boy's face.

Still nothing.

In the cold hum of the air-conditioning, three orderlies entered. They stared at the boy breathing slowly at their feet.

Perhaps it was the warm air rushing in from the open door, the scent of men cutting through the room's cleaning fluid, or a whisper that warned David something was happening. He raised his head, sharpened his gaze into the vacant haze, and in a moment of clarity, shoved his palms against the floor and pushed against the wall in an attempt to stand, to gain a footing.

He only slid lower.

The orderlies stepped closer.

"Get a move on," a security guard snapped from the door.

With a yank, David's head cracked against the floor. The attendants in their white uniforms propped him upright. Half standing like a teenager after his first long night in a bar, David fell into the sober ones, who pushed him the few feet toward the door.

Laughter roared down the hall. Rows of adolescents hollered at the boy they'd known for only a few weeks.

"Come on, David, throw a punch! Kick the fat ass!" an older voice screamed.

A smaller boy shouted, "Bite 'em in the arm!"

Another boy stripped to his underwear danced into the path, mimicking David's neck lopping from side to side. "I spit at that one, there, in his fuckin' face!" he gloated.

The clearing narrowed. Stumbling in the hallway, the orderlies and a security guard yanked the limp body upward. The shouts grew. McCowell slammed the bar on the stairwell's door. The exit drifted shut behind them and the uproar quieted. David was alone with the staff.

The wrap of men navigated the narrow stairs and lowered the teenager cautiously, aware that a tumble would bring them all down. At the last of the three flights, the rush down the steps must have been tempting, an end to the claustrophobia and to the freedom of the open night. The tangle loosened around the boy. Guards peeled away, hunched and sweating, grateful for the evening cool and the stars that burned the black heaven above.

On the concrete landing, David stood separate from all he knew, all he trusted. A mere month had taught him that no one was there to help. He could take the chance to bolt. He'd run for the fences and hide in the woods. He'd think which way to his parents' house, 225 miles southwest in Foley. But by the time David took his best guess, the dogs from the Ventress men's prison in Clayton would've been set loose. Bred to chase and snare, the pack would circle, leap, then snap at his neck until it tore him to the ground. A trooper or guard would drag him by the head and shove him into an Alabama state car. Running would only give him a few hours. He'd be back.

McCowell nodded to the others. The men recircled, dragging David across the gravel road that divided the institution until they reached a warehouse against the barbed-wire perimeter fencing. McCowell broke off, jerked open a door that read VOCATIONAL REHABILITATION. Under the glare of industrial lights, worktables and stools were scattered where children at the facility ripped apart strings of rubber fishing lures, stuffing them in plastic baggies for the tourists and tackle shops in town. Past the workspace was an office door that was always shut. McCowell pulled a key from his belt. At the sight of the darkened, unfamiliar room, David flailed against the men around him. The Thorazine was clearing his system. "Mom? Dad? Where are you?" he howled at the corrugated roof.

The men were football player big, and there were a lot of them. This worked against them as they crushed against each other in the shadows. A slick arm elbowed a gut. A foot scraped a shin. Scrambling to hold the boy in their core, the man closest yelled at McCowell, "The fucking door! Get the fuckin' thing open!"

McCowell moved to the nearest of three black metal doors. Fumbling to free the wooden crossbar from its brackets, he threw it to the ground and glanced over his shoulder in the dim light. A trail of abandoned Christmas lights spidered out of a box. *Why can't that goddamned kid shut up?* With everything he had, McCowell pressed the pit of his palm against the latch pin until the metal door gave way. Inside, the cell was smeared with red mud as high as a child could reach. A mesh of steel was bolted overhead. Over that, a single bulb burned. The stench of urine and feces wafted from the corners.

A guard lifted David from the muddy floor, while others pushed from behind. The boy hit the ground in a lurching heave as the men rushed for the exit. They knew he'd throw himself at the door with all he had, and they couldn't let him escape. McCowell snapped the lock shut, slid the latch pin back, and wedged the crossbar into place. No one acknowledged the screams.

David Dolihite had been admitted to the Eufaula Adolescent Center only a few weeks earlier on January 13, 1992. He came from Foley in Baldwin County, not far from Mobile Bay. David was the second oldest of five children, the only boy among four girls. His family lived in a neighborhood of single-story brick homes, double-wide trailers, and gravelly front yards. Chain-link fences separated families. His dad, like other dads, owned a truck. Satellite TV dishes spread like morning glories in Foley. Conversations with neighbors were friendly but short. People kept to themselves and to their own. David's middle-aged parents worked hard for everything they had. His father was the custodian at the local high school. His mother managed the deli counter at the Winn-Dixie.

David never won a science award or came home with a glowing report card. He wasn't much for sports. Family, not friends, came to his birthday parties. He liked heroes and rebels and imagined himself as one. He spoke up for the weaker kids, sometimes defending them with his fists. With teachers, he went from quiet to rude. He got a reputation. The smallest mistake—a forgotten piece of homework, a moment of talking in class—was labeled unacceptable, insolent, or rude. He was tagged as a kid who didn't matter; certainly, not one to be forgiven. Suspended for cursing at a teacher and confined to home by the school's order, he snuck out for the afternoon. It was a mistake that would haunt the Dolihites. That was when the principal grabbed his chance to force David and his parents into juvenile court. The Baldwin County judge said that a stint at the state institution would do David good.

Eufaula was Alabama's largest mental institution for children, with psychiatric treatment designed for kids who had a problem with rules. Mom and Dad resisted for nearly a year, until a state official from Eufaula called the house. She promised a mental health summer camp with horses, bikes, and a pool—everything a teenager would love. The best and highest treatment was available, she claimed. "As you're aware, the judge has decided that this is in your son's *best* interest." When David's parents wouldn't buy it, the woman turned on them. The boy was going with or without their approval. Their son's ride to Eufaula had already been arranged. The only question was whether they gave their consent and allowed his admission to be labeled "voluntary." They would learn that voluntary didn't count for much—a fact they would learn about Eufaula too late.

The Dolihites loved their son. They found therapists, and together they drove David down to Mobile, where he sat in sessions with and without them. Then the insurance money ran out. They attended meetings with high school teachers and principals, patiently listening to the need for stricter discipline and how they, as parents, could be better. They went to church and asked for the minister's advice. The well-intentioned pastor advised prayer groups and better Sunday attendance. With no choice and nothing else to do, Mom and Dad said, *Yes, okay*. They loved David desperately. They surrendered him to Eufaula.

The family never saw the institution. As much as they hadn't liked the woman who called, she worked with the state mental health department, so she must've known what she was doing. As David's father put it to his wife, "She was an expert." Neither he nor his wife imagined that the woman was a barefaced liar.

Chapter Two

Looking over my résumé in his small office, in an oversize pair of cargo shorts, the nonprofit's legal director flipped to the second page. I was dressed in an Armani suit and polished loafers with a brass-lock briefcase beside me.

"We asked for a senior litigator from public interest, not a junior corporate associate in a private firm." The man, Jerry Taubman, dropped my résumé on his desk.

"Yes, the woman from Harvard's career office let me know that."

"Trial briefs?"

"No."

"Depositions?"

"None."

"Have you drafted a discovery request, an interrogatory, or a document production?" I rubbed the back of my neck, worried

I was already missing work at the firm. “No, except for clerking during the summer before I graduated.”

Taubman and I both knew that was hardly legal experience.

The firm had given me assignments over those eight weeks, between sending me to Dodgers games and taking me to dinners at LA’s high-toned restaurants. I swam at the LA Country Club, where Howard Hughes had clipped the golf course’s trees trying out a plane he had promised the army. And I was paid a lawyer’s full salary. All of that came with the summer. Firms did it to recruit new lawyers like me.

Taubman had graduated from Harvard Law School twelve years before I had. That’s where our commonality ended. He hadn’t gone to a private firm. Instead, he had clerked for Alabama federal judge Frank Johnson, the man known for single-handedly enforcing desegregation across the state. Taubman went on to be a staff attorney at the Southern Poverty Law Center. He was now the legal director of the Bazelon Center, which specialized in defending the constitutional rights of individuals confined to psychiatric hospitals.

“Have you even been inside a courtroom?” Taubman was sounding more and more incredulous.

“Yes.”

“Well, would you like to share?”

I watched as he dropped his yellow pad and stopped taking notes. He had plenty of work to do once he was finished with me, and I was shaping up to be a complete waste of his time.

With my head straight and voice steady, I answered as if I were reciting a case in law school. Only this time, the case was my own. “The dispute involved the county of Los Angeles versus my twenty-four-year-old mother. The stated claim was that a paranoid schizophrenic had neglected her six, well, almost seven-year-old son. Applying California Welfare and Institutions Code Section 300, the court found in favor of the county, removing her custody over the boy and granting the county the right to separate them. The proceeding took about five minutes; the separation lasted eleven and a half years."

That wasn't everything. I left out the psychiatric institutions where my mom, Hope, was a patient: Camarillo State Mental Hospital, Metropolitan State Hospital, and her last, Arizona State Hospital. At least, those were the ones I knew of. I didn't mention MacLaren Hall, the institution where I was sent for a year after being taken from her. Operated by the county of Los Angeles, the walled and caged compound could pack in three hundred boys and girls from newborns to eighteen-year-olds. Thousands followed me after I left. The violence inside was sudden and random. Grand juries, newspaper accounts, and reports from children arrived at the same conclusion: shut it down. Los Angeles refused to listen. Children were still being sent there.

Taubman's skepticism about my suitability for the position was understandable.

When I'd called the law school's career office three weeks earlier, the woman on the phone had been slightly more encouraging. I was at my desk early as usual. "Are you unhappy where you are?" she'd asked. I answered that I was okay. "Has the firm done something we should know about?" she pressed. Then before I could reply, she added that leaving a job so soon wouldn't look good on a résumé. I closed my door and reassured her, "I'm just wondering about other openings." She asked what area, and I said children, maybe foster care.

There was a public-interest firm in Washington, DC, she said, acting as lead counsel in a federal class action. The lawsuit, *Wyatt v. Stickney,* covered every Alabama psychiatric institution. Children were kept at a remote facility called Eufaula. Some were in foster care or likely to enter it. The position was for two years.

"The job pays in the low twenties," the woman said. "That can't be a fifth of what you're making. I guess you could defer your student loans." She seemed at a loss. "But you'd still have to move. Are you really interested?"

"Yes, I'd like to apply," I answered. "What else do you know?"

She replied that the state of Alabama allegedly had kept children in cages or some kind of cells. "Children have been hurt inside the institution," she said.

That phone call with the woman had been one thing; sitting across from Taubman now was another. I brought up the cells. The room went quiet. Taubman looked straight at me.

Apparently, what I said was enough to keep him from ending the interview entirely. He leaned back and added a few more facts. There was the children's facility at Eufaula, but there was also Alabama's constellation of seven adult psychiatric hospitals, a surprising number for a state of that size. Added to that were five developmental centers—formerly known as residential "schools and hospitals"—for people of any age, and of course, the publicly run nursing facilities scattered across the state.

"There was a mention of children being hurt?" I asked.

The question caught Taubman off guard. He took a minute.

Alabama had acquired an abandoned military base on the outskirts of the City of Eufaula to stop housing children directly with adults in psychiatric units. Every child there was from age twelve to eighteen. The facility handled children with behavioral problems but who weren't psychotic or otherwise mentally ill. They were the kids who talked back, skipped school, snuck out at night, or broke family rules. Nearly all of them came from working families across the state.

One boy had committed suicide earlier that year. Another had tried to hang himself and suffered permanent brain damage. No one knew what happened to the family of the child who died. The one who survived had been sent back to his parents. That boy's name was David Dolihite.

Folding my résumé in half, Taubman politely smiled. "You're one of the first to be interviewed. I'll get back to you," he said. I picked up my briefcase, thanked him for his time, and left.

Chapter Three

Mom never saw the inside of a university lecture hall. She had found her school in the back of the newspaper classified ads. About a half mile from where we lived in North Hollywood, the Page Beauty School promised a "lifetime career" with low tuition on "EZ terms." Dog-eared copies of *Vogue, Glamour,* and *Cosmopolitan* were Hope's textbooks.

Hope was the mother the other moms stared at. She was too young and pretty and wore a tight orange miniskirt with thigh-high boots. A great look for a cocktail bar, but not for collecting her son from first grade. Each morning, she dressed me for school, tucking my shirt in around my hips. "You mind your teachers. You be a good boy. You stand up for yourself." On weekends, she and I would watch as hippies in alleys made candles out of buckets of sand. Red, yellow, orange, the smell of wax simmering in coffee cans. Barefoot and dirty, sitting cross-legged, they ignored us until Hope handed one a quarter. I carried that candle home.

There was always something a little wrong. The way she had to make a brave boy out of me, sending me back outside to face down a neighborhood bully who wouldn't leave me alone. It was my problem, she said. If a score needed to be settled, her boy was going to be the one to do it. Mothers get their children ready for the world, for the world that they know. Hope's world had too much risk and not enough luck. And then she just broke.

Hope told me that I was being hunted. A pack of men was out roaming the streets, and I was the one they wanted to catch. She'd flatten her palms against the windows arguing with men that didn't exist, yelling she'd kill them if they touched the front door.

She took me to a Saturday matinee not long before I was taken from her. I had stopped trusting that she'd be back if she left me. I kept thinking she'd get lost or forget me.

"You'll like it, I promise. Just be quiet," she said. I was six and acting like a baby.

"I want to stay with you, Mom," I said.

She bought a ticket. Just one. She gave the attendant her money, a handful of change wrapped in a dollar bill, then yanked me by the arm from behind her skirt.

"He likes Coke and Good & Plenty's," she snapped at the teenager. "What's your name? This is Andy." I kept squirming from her grip.

"I'm Gary." He couldn't have been more than sixteen.

Hope's hands dug into my shoulders. Then, turning to the boy, she said, "Just take him." Before he could say anything, she left.

At the concession stand, Gary asked for a Coke, then the candy. He added a popcorn on his own, just a kid in his pressed white shirt and narrow black tie. Arcade lights ran across the ceiling.

"You wanna hold my hand?" he offered awkwardly. I didn't. He carried everything into the theater and stopped at the edge of a dark row. I climbed up into the seat.

"It's starting soon, don't worry," he whispered.

He tucked the popcorn and candy beside my leg and crouched down to get the Coke. His shirt sleeves were pitted with sweat. His feet were massive in those shiny shoes, ones that he could have only worn for work. I remember the smell of rancid butter and cigarettes.

"Can you hold on to that?" he asked. The cold wax cup slid into my hands. "All set," he said with a nod. Then I sat, my feet dangling in the dark, waiting for the gray screen to light up.

I liked the movie from the start. Two dirty kids my age were skipping school. A rich lady with a frilly hat picked them up on the side of the road, and when she drove them home and confronted their father, he told her to mind her own business. Mom was like that, yelling at people to leave us alone.

Then just as it was getting going, it ended. The screen went blank, and the lights went on. My row was empty, and there was no one to tell me what to do. Didn't make much sense, but that's how it was. I bundled up my popcorn and walked outside.

"Mom, where are you?" I whispered.

I sat on the curb and looked down the empty block. I did my best. Then everything just busted open. I began pacing in front of the booth, crying that she had left me. I was a problem. "Aggravating" was the word she'd used. I didn't know what it meant, but I knew that I wasn't good enough, that I made her want to go. This was all on me. This was my fault. I wrapped my arms around my belly. Then Gary rushed out and explained that the movie wasn't over. It hadn't ended, it was just intermission. "It's not finished," he said. "Hurry up, you'll miss the end." He pulled me back inside and handed me another full Coke from the counter.

"You haven't missed that much," he whispered.

"Where's my mom?" I asked.

Someone shushed us from behind.

"I'm sure she'll be here when the movie ends," he promised with his hand on my shoulder.

I unrolled my bag of popcorn and grabbed a fistful.

This thin, smiling man was on the screen now, tiptoeing across an old village square with a long nose and black gloves, bells jingling.

"Children, where are you? I know you're here somewhere," he said with a curled smile.

Free lollipops and pies were waiting. Anything they wanted was theirs inside his clown-decorated carriage. The boy and girl listened from the basement window. He gave up and was dancing out of view. They were still tempted.

Don't go, don't follow him, I kept thinking. *They'll take you like Mom said.*

They couldn't help themselves. They ran out, waving for him to stop. The carriage halted and the man sighed, relieved that he hadn't lost his touch. He swung round at them with sickly yellow eyes.

"Come to me, come to me," he repeated, lowering the wooden ramp. Everything delicious was just inches away inside the gold-curtained door.

"He's lying. Can't you see that?" I whispered. "They do that."

They crept up the ramp, and the child catcher shoved them inside. The carriage's gold-and-purple trimmings fell to the road, revealing a cage. The children grabbed at the prison bars. He swung up to the front and whipped at his horse. The boy and girl disappeared with him down the street.

When the movie ended, I walked outside. As my eyes adjusted to the glare of the sidewalk, fear turned to relief when I picked out Mom waiting there impatiently. As we walked home, I yammered on about the movie, the magical car, the happy ending. I never said anything about getting confused, about leaving early and crying on the curb. Nothing about children being abducted, held endlessly in an underground prison.

Mom had to have asked me a question or two, just to show that she was listening. By then, she had warned me about strangers taking me from her. She had been in foster care and spent time in a girls' home. "You need to be ready," she warned with hollow eyes, "because someone may come to take you." I didn't know she had grown up dirt poor. She and her younger brother had gone in and out of children's homes across Colorado. I wouldn't have understood what she meant if she had told me.

But she was changing. Before, the strangers she talked about were policemen or someone from the county, but now she was warning me about men on the hunt for a boy like me. They were like that one man in his carriage searching neighborhoods, snatching up children from wherever their parents hid them. It made the two of us so close and alone. "Someday, they'll take you away and drown you in a barrel." For her and then for me, the child catcher was real. She didn't know she was a young woman beginning her psychotic breaks. I didn't know I was a boy watching his mother lose her mind.

Then our child catcher came. And she tore Mom and me apart.

Of all my social workers, there had to be a first one. She was a "detention worker," and her job was the rawest in the system. She couldn't have gone into the field wanting to do that kind of work. No one did. She didn't handle cases or visit kids in their homes. There was no sitting down with a mother and her child, listening to what had broken and how their existence had spun so utterly out of control. There were no more questions. The time for listening was over. The decision had been made. Her only task was to go out and take children from their parents. If she did it right, she'd do it quickly.

It was the week before my seventh birthday when that first social worker shoved me into her car outside a seedy North Hollywood motel. I've long since forgotten her name. I doubt she remembered mine. It wasn't her responsibility to know much about us, a few details from a case file summary that she'd been handed—a boy wasn't attending school, his mother had run-ins with the police, a neighbor reported that something didn't seem right.

Hope fought for me on the sidewalk, wrapping her body around my bony frame. With the help of a sheriff's deputy, the woman yanked me from Mom's arms. Then she hustled me into the front seat of her car. We left Hope where she was, screaming in the morning sun. As we were fleeing the scene, the woman kept telling me not to cry. We were headed to a nice place, she promised, somewhere there'd be other children just like me.

That nice place was an abandoned polio hospital that LA County had turned into MacLaren Hall. We approached the perimeter, with its fourteen-foot chain-link fence and spooled barbed wire with floodlights that came on after dark. The woman yelled into a call box that she had a drop-off. The gate opened slowly. Inside the derelict admission hall, she bickered with the clerk over my missing file. I clung to that woman, begging her not to go.

What was now MacLaren Hall was once the Sister Kenny Polio Hospital, which opened in 1950. With the discovery of a polio vaccine, the hospital was shuttered in less than a decade. The county's probation department bought the dormant facility in 1959. It wasn't the best spot for a children's shelter, but as a bureaucrat told the local papers, there was "no other place where the county could get this much bed space at so cheap a price."

With too many children and too few foster families, the question of where to put a taken child had been a problem for years. MacLaren seemed like the answer. The whole point was to stop sending foster children to the overrun wards of juvenile hall, where children were victimizing children and those who had already been abused or neglected weren't much of a match for guards. The county never followed through on its plan.

That ten-acre tract on LA's dusty outskirts became a charnel house of childhoods.

Taken from their parents, children were thrown together inside MacLaren's "maximum security" and wired windows. Every foster child was called an inmate. "The beds may all be full," a reporter commented, "but there's always room for one more—and maybe another and another." He had that right. The processing of children was cattle-like. Dropped off, a child was interviewed in his street clothes, stripped and weighed, given a "thorough bath," and issued MacLaren-stenciled shirts and pants before being escorted to a sleeping ward. When it was finally over, the child had been handed off to six different strangers. From the start, the county barred the children from attending the local schools, and whatever education they got was provided on-site, away from the general public. There weren't enough teachers, and those who did work there were paid less than their colleagues elsewhere. Equipment was poor, and lessons were taught in overcrowded, loud classrooms. Children's schooling was not a priority.

Four years after MacLaren opened, grand jury investigators drove out to get a good look. When they returned, they recommended razing the place to the ground. They reported that conditions inside MacLaren were actually worse than facilities for juvenile offenders. Elected officials answered that budgets were tight. Voters wrote to newspapers that money was already being wasted. The year after I left, taxpayers rejected the third ballot measure to pay for improvements. If a child was lucky, the stay would be around a month. A child labeled "non-placeable" could linger there for years, left in squalor.

According to my MacLaren Hall school records, I was there for one year nearly to the day. The timing struck me as odd. I had stopped talking. I had withdrawn into nothing inside MacLaren's chaotic wards. I did as I was told. But a seven-year-old who had gone mute was less of a chore among MacLaren's child inmates. I was a problem that could wait.

The months ground on, through the summer and the first half of second grade. With the end of the holidays, my file popped up for its annual review. Layered thick with orderlies, industrial upkeep, guards, and administrators, MacLaren didn't run cheap. My year was up, and with an eye toward keeping costs in check, a county placement committee did its work and moved me into a more affordable foster home. The timing was bureaucratic homework.

But my first day has remained one of my sharpest memories. Hours after the detention worker left me, the orderlies had already stripped me twice. First out of my street clothes, then again for my physical examination. I had only been naked in front of Mom. I was too frightened to be stripped again for the gang showers. One of the staff dragged me through the corridors and into what had been a hospital basement. He unlocked a dark room and left me there. That was my first taste of going missing with no one coming to get me. I still dread elevators, locked cars, and rooms without lights.

Chapter Four

David Dolihite had already been at Eufaula for a month when conditions there came to the attention of Alabama's top mental health official. Royce King was a successful businessman with no experience in medicine or mental health when the governor put him in charge of Alabama's sprawling network of mental institutions, including the Eufaula Adolescent Center. Even in horse-trading politics, King's appointment as the state's commissioner of mental health raised eyebrows. His position was a plum, putting him in the governor's cabinet and at the heart of power. But the Department of Mental Health was known for being rife with cronyism, and King's manifest unsuitability for the job was ignored.

Kathy Sawyer was the department's lead investigator for every case involving harm done to patients in the system. After King's appointment, he became Sawyer's new boss, but fortunately,

Sawyer was no crony. She warned King about what was going on at Eufaula via an internal memo. No doubt aware of King's complete lack of clinical training, Sawyer went straight to the point:

> I am writing to bring to your attention again our concerns about the Eufaula Adolescent Center. As you know, we have reported over the years several concerns regarding clinical practices and other treatments of this population as follows:
>
> – inappropriate use of time-out and seclusion;
> – use of fire extinguishers and fire hoses instead of mace;
> – adolescents sodomizing each other while in time-out unknowing to staff;
> – adolescents sodomizing each other during bathing, bedtimes, etc., again unknowingly to staff.
>
> I am asking you to intervene immediately and take necessary steps.... I cannot impress upon you the disservice to those placed in this facility for mental health care and treatment, not to mention the vulnerable and liable situation the Department faces with these non-therapeutic practices.

When later questioned under oath, King stated that he wasn't familiar with Eufaula's admission criteria for children. Notwithstanding the clear implications in the memo from Sawyer, he claimed he wasn't aware that staff was forbidden from locking a child in a seclusion room for punishment, so he did nothing to stop it. When reports like Sawyer's documenting abusive conditions at Eufaula came across his desk, he admitted that he did "scan those." Then he feebly protested that he was ill-equipped to understand the reports and simply relied on the hope that others would handle any problems.

So Royce King went about his job in a vacuum of ignorance, managing the department budget and believing that his oversight ensured the money was being spent wisely. But as one federal judge concluded, he seemed to have no idea if what was spent improved services at Eufaula or was woefully off the mark. Despite being the top mental health policymaker in the state, King deflected any responsibility for the harm done to David Dolihite by claiming, without irony, that he was unqualified for his job in the first place.

King left his position as Alabama's commissioner of mental health in 1993 but incredibly was later given another post with the department. As reported in the press, the then newly elected governor told his chief of staff to find something for King, and soon thereafter, one of the state's facilities for people with developmental disabilities hired him. King told reporters that he didn't feel that his friendship with the governor had anything to do with getting the job. The annual salary was $26,000, somewhat on the low side given King's success in business. That left the question of what it was all about. The chief of staff cleared it up after resigning from his post. King was given the job because he needed the health benefits.

Chapter Five

Mom was confined to the Arizona State Hospital for nearly seven years. It was the last of her psychiatric placements. Called to a squalid motel, Phoenix police officers found her in her room. She was curled against the wall, emaciated and filthy, whispering bits of incomprehensible thoughts. No one knew how she had gotten there from Los Angeles. Since her first psychotic break, which I had witnessed as a boy, Hope had spent nearly twenty years in mental institutions.

When Mom arrived, hospital administrators assigned her to the institution's "Juniper Complex," its own hive of ten interconnected lockdown wings, with a mix of civilly committed men and women. Involuntary commitments were climbing, but no one seemed to want the work of watching, cleaning up after, and feeding patients. New hires were getting tougher and tougher to find.

There simply wasn't enough staff to handle every overcrowded ward. Mom was in the largest diagnostic grouping, termed "Schizophrenic Disorders." Her bed was in Juniper-Four, which had its own admissions criteria:

> Female; 35 to 65 years of age; no major acute medical problems; ambulatory; behavior is influenced by either delusions or hallucinations; impairment in functions in several areas; requires supervision or assistance to maintain personal hygiene; may physically attack others with intent to harm; may be self-abusive.

I told myself that I should've called more often, but when I did call from the East Coast, when I did finally reach her in the human warehouse that was Juniper-Four, our conversations went the same:

> *Mom, how are you? It's Andy.*
>
> *I'm fine.*
>
> *Is it hot there in Phoenix? Do you remember that I'm in law school outside Boston?*
>
> *I know.*
>
> *Do you have anything you need? Can I send you something?*
>
> *No.*
>
> *Are you sure? Some money, maybe a purse?*

No.

I love you, Mom.

Thank you.

All right, I'll call you again.

Then in the spring semester before my graduation from law school, Arizona's Supreme Court ruled that the state was obligated to do much more for indigent people with chronic mental illness. People had a right to live outside the state hospital's locked grounds. That didn't mean dumping them on the street—the court was clear about that—it meant paying for their care in the community. But even before that with the state hospital beds overflowing into hallways, bureaucrats had grudgingly begun emptying the decrepit wards.

Mom had met the hospital's criteria for discharge: "Patients are discharged directly from J-Four when their behavior is appropriate and acceptable in boarding homes, structured supervisory care settings, or nursing homes." Hope was placed in a state-contracted boarding home called The Ability Lodge.

While Hope was being moved to her boarding home, I was settling into my first job at a Los Angeles law firm—Manatt, Phelps, Rothenberg & Phillips. The firm was brash compared to its East Coast competitors. The lawyers had a political bent; partners were close friends with Bill Clinton; several were confidants to Governor Brown and several US senators. It had one of Hollywood's best entertainment practices—music and film were strong suits. The offices were modern and sleek, inspiring the TV series *L.A. Law*.

I had previously clerked at the firm and was now one of its new hires. The firm spared no expense on salaries and perks for start-up associates. The younger lawyers had assigned parking spots in the basement, filled with gleaming BMWs and Mercedes. The firm had gone all in on the two-story library, complete with a stunning view of downtown. The rooftop basketball court and private gym were perfect for lunch breaks. I did my best, hoping that my best would do. I rushed to partners' offices for assignments and sat across from them with a practiced smile. I couldn't have gotten any further from where I had come from and what I remembered as a boy growing up.

Chapter Six

"Do you know which part of this is supposed to be treatment?" One boy asked that of an expert touring his Eufaula ward. The thirteen-year-old's unfiltered words had taken the woman aback. He was a younger patient in a facility that took children aged twelve and up. The expert didn't record his name or her answer, though she later wrote the boy had been there only a few days and had already been repeatedly secluded by staff.

Lawyers for Alabama's psychiatric patients sent her to the isolated facility and asked her to report back on what she found. They chose her because she had run a state psychiatric facility for children, meaning she knew her way around places like Eufaula.

From conversations with children, she determined that most suffered from depression, anxiety, suicidal thoughts, guilt, and low self-esteem. Many children were using those very words to describe themselves. They seemed to possess extraordinarily high levels of what clinical psychiatrists called "insight," that being a patient's ability to recognize their own mental illness. What struck her as odd was the mechanical manner in how children said it. They were reciting the exact phrases each time—as if she had asked them to recite the Pledge of Allegiance or Boy Scout's honor code out of the blue.

Going through children's charts, she found that half had no treatment plan at all. The treatment plans that did exist were virtually identical from child to child. They were copied templates with the same one- or two-word catchphrases stamped out for every child. Few contained a diagnosis of a child's actual problems or offered a targeted strategy to address them. When she spoke with children, they weren't demonstrating psychiatric insight; they were repeating the same generic codes that staff had assigned them. As much as she hunted, there was no evidence of tailored therapy that a locked mental facility was professionally expected to provide.

What she found was punishment. Staff enforced regular "lockdowns," restricting children to their wards and rooms for weeks. They went through "head counts" three to four times a day. Staff described children who ran away as having "broken out." Dogs from a nearby prison were used to hunt them down.

Eufaula ran on a hierarchy of rewards and punishments that determined what a child could and could not do. It sounded reasonable at first. At the highest rank, children were entitled to recreational and therapeutic activities. At the lowest, they were confined to their bunk or, if necessary, one of the seclusion rooms. The result was devastating.

Combing through children's seclusion reports, the attorney's expert found that staff isolated more than half of Eufaula's children at any given time. The ranking system also enforced the most glaring racial disparities: on the day the expert arrived, she located only one Black child, male or female, whom staff had assigned any higher than the lowest.

Staff essentially punished children until they stopped being depressed. Every new incident involving a child required more confinement. It became a tightening grip of seclusion. A child's isolation went from two to three, then five days, until it was counted in weeks. And when the wards' seclusion rooms were deemed ineffective, staff moved children's punishment to the three jail cells that had once comprised the brig when the property was one of the largest military bases on the southern coast.

Before leaving, she observed another boy's arrival, something every child went through. "We went downstairs," she wrote, "and I watched as a staff person in the admissions office 'processed' the boy. She never introduced herself to him. She never really spoke to him, except to ask specific questions off a form. She made no effort to welcome him and gave no indication that she was aware of this boy's nervousness about being in a new place. Nothing about the way this boy was treated during his admission to Eufaula was designed, intended, or had the effect of reassuring him that he was in a safe, nurturing, humane treatment environment."

She reported back that it was one of the emptiest things she'd ever seen.

Chapter Seven

It was an early afternoon on Friday when I left work to visit Mom. I got up from my office desk and slipped down to the elevators without telling anyone. Dodging through freeway traffic to LAX, I imagined her smiling when she saw me. I hadn't called ahead.

The room at the Phoenix Hilton was large, with a bedroom and seating area. Mom and I could drive around, then come here for room service and a movie. I dropped my duffel bag on the bed and reached for the phone. Suddenly, I regretted not getting her permission to come.

The first ring went on forever until I hung up. I tried again, and a man's slurred voice answered. "May I speak with Hope Bridge—I'm sorry, I mean Priscilla. Would you tell her it's Andrew?" I hesitated, aware the voice that had answered still hadn't gone beyond hello. "No, tell her Andy, her son."

In a nod to her Pentecostal upbringing, she named me Andrew, the first of the apostles with his brother Peter. Putting "Andy" down on my birth certificate, that was her rebellion against that same upbringing. Our names had changed while we were apart. Institutions had renamed both of us. Harvard gave me "Andrew." When I applied as Andy, I must have sounded like a hayseed or a kid thinking he was clever and trying to stand out. The registrar's office corrected it, so I became Andrew on the seating charts and campus mail. When a law professor yelled it out across the lecture hall, it took only a second for me to give up the name that Mom gave me. A clerk must've changed Hope's name, too. Someone on the admissions unit of a psychiatric hospital had decided her middle name wouldn't do, and Hope was now Priscilla.

I heard a sharp *whack* and imagined the receiver of one of those mounted phones banging against a wall. A racket of voices and a TV spat through the line. When Mom said hello, there was a gauziness in her tone. I thought of her eyes adjusting to see who had woken her. Her voice sounded older than it should have. By my count, she was forty-two.

"Mom, it's Andy. I'm here, not far from where you are. I've rented a car."

"You're in Phoenix?" Her breathing was heavy.

"Yes, I'm here. Just uptown. It'll take me thirty minutes to get there." I waited. "I'll see you then." Before she could answer, possibly refuse, I hung up.

The collection of ranch-style bungalows sat well apart from its neighbors. A chain-link fence, broken in places, wrapped through the dirt. Beside an aluminum-sided camping trailer, Hope waited in the sun.

There were unavoidable practicalities to consider before becoming what the state called a "community provider"—a group home where psychiatric patients could be put after being discharged. An operator took the state's mandatory course and then the test for the operating license. The family dining room wasn't big enough in typical residential homes, and a cafeteria-style eating area would have to be built. Kitchens needed enlarging to accommodate industrial-size refrigerators and ovens, plus the storage areas for the discount food. By the time every building code and mandated staffing ratio was met, it was like any small business: the owner had to figure out how to cover costs.

Eking out even a modest profit required increasing the only source of revenue—paying customers. This meant adding more beds for the psychiatric patients the state decided to hand over to fill them. It also meant mediocre care. Operators had to be savvy, or they'd soon go belly-up. A bevy of connected homes would be snapped up, usually in the poorest and cheapest parts of town. There was another advantage to that: people in those neighborhoods were less likely to complain when patients started moving in.

"Mom, it's me, Andy."

Her head was twitching while she rolled her tongue inside her mouth. Her hair was closely shaved, stubbled with black. She glanced in my direction, as if she were struggling to remember why she was waiting in the heat. Not a word came back from her.

"Do you like your hair that way?" I asked. As a kid, I had spent hours looking at her bathroom reflection while she adjusted her boyish haircut. The edgy style was parted at the right, then lacquered with sweeps of Alberto VO5 that she took from the salon where she worked.

She dropped her head and whispered something. I tapped her shoulder, and thinking she wouldn't want a hug, I touched the sweatshirt that hung to her long pants. Across from my suede lace-ups were her worn running shoes. She had left them untied, covering her feet like a pair of slippers.

"Are you hungry?" she blankly asked. "They're having dessert." A Styrofoam bowl of yellow pudding rested in the well of a plastic chair. "Would you like it?"

"I'm not much for desserts." I gazed at the metal gate. "Maybe we can head inside out of the heat."

"It's banana," she continued. I interrupted and reached for the bowl. "Let's go inside, Mom."

She led the way into a boarded-up and cracked patio. The heat was saturated with the smell of human bodies and spoiled food. A ceiling-mounted television was set to an afternoon game show, the volume reduced to a trace. Behind me was the blown-open entrance to what appeared to have been the former living room expanded to include whatever rooms had been around it. Hope ignored the residents watching from the slumped sofa, a few off to the corner in folding chairs. They ignored her.

Lingering at a screen door, Mom stared out at the sunlight. I leaned to another woman who I guessed was older than my mother. Not wanting to go back outside yet, I squatted on my heels. "My name's Andy. Hope, I mean Priscilla, over there is my mom." The woman's chin lifted and her eyes focused. The corners of her mouth were crusted with dry skin.

"Would you like this?" I held out the pudding and balanced the bowl on her bare knee.

"Yes, thank you." She pulled the dessert closer to her belly, then shifted toward my mother's figure in the sunlight. "I didn't know Priscilla had a friend."

Reaching over Mom's head, I pushed open the screen door. She paced past a row of clapboard cabins. A water pipe rested in the sun.

"Can we go to your room, Mom?" I asked, stepping up to her side. "Do you have roommates?"

Without answering, she went on ahead.

"Do you like it here? Do you have friends?"

She said nothing.

To the side of the main house, she stopped at an unlocked plywood shed. We stepped inside, where an overhead fan circled the heat. Pressed against the corner was a wooden bed frame supporting a twin mattress topped with a Mickey Mouse comforter. Plastic and stuffed toys toppled across the dresser. A baby bottle rested on the nightstand. The one plastered wall, which I assumed was part of the main house, was spread with pages ripped from teen magazines—the ones for sale in the cashier lines at Safeway.

"Mom, would you like to sit down?" I smoothed out the bedcover.

She rolled her tongue around her mouth again, pushing out her bottom lip. Eyes ahead, she sat beside me. I wrapped my hand around her yellow-stained fingertips. She had always smoked. She slipped her hand away.

"Do you want a toy?" She shuffled toward the dresser.

"Yes, of course, Mom. Thanks."

She opened the dresser drawer with a yank that surprised me.

"Do you remember that stuffed elephant you brought me for my birthday?" I asked. "It was at the foster home. I think I was eight, or was it nine? It was right before—" I cut myself short before I said *you disappeared.*

She dug into the drawer and said nothing.

"Your birthday is coming up," I remarked. "It's a Tuesday this year."

She dug into another corner while I watched.

"Here." She dropped a key ring beside me. A hard rubber Tweety Bird and Sylvester dangled from its chain. I squeezed the pair of them and felt Tweety's feet digging into my palm.

"Would you like to come back to the hotel?" I asked. "We could watch a movie. You can order something if you want. Or go for a walk outside."

Hope tapped the edge of her jaw with her forefinger, twisted her neck, and giggled.

"Is there somewhere you'd like to go?" I asked. "Would they let me take you?"

"There's the gas station," she offered.

Hope knew the way—the Circle K station was straight up the street. When we got there, I bent to tie her shoelace, and she shifted her foot from my grasp.

"Mom." I glanced up from the searing pavement. "Mom, please stop staring at the sun."

She halted at the gas pumps. I guided her closer but she resisted. She muttered softly, and when I leaned against her to hear it again, she said something about the owner banning her from his store.

"I'll be right back, Mom."

The blast of freezing air shot down through my shirt. Gazing into the showcase refrigerator, I'd forgotten to ask what she drank.

I grabbed two Evian bottles and walked up to the girl behind the counter. I paid for the water and a carton of Parliaments.

Looking out at the awning, I saw the lot was empty. She wasn't where I'd left her. I ran out to the intersection, looked in every direction, and saw nothing. In the hot reek of drying gasoline, I dropped the bag at my feet. I had lost her again.

A car pulled in, and as a young woman headed toward the pump, her little girl ran out toward the store. She halted, and I looked at her as she looked at Hope, who now was resting on the knee-high wall. "Don't you stare at her," her mother yelled. "Get your candy and get back here."

Our backs to the desert, Hope and I watched the woman fumble with the hose. I pulled out a pack of cigarettes and handed her one. When I reached into my pocket for the matches, she shook her head.

"I'll light it, Andy."

I tried to make a joke. "You ever think about quitting? Those things will kill you."

"I traded cigarettes for smoking pot."

"You smoke pot, Mom?" The moment became so ordinary, just another mom telling her grown-up son an old secret about herself.

"Not anymore, I didn't like it," she corrected me. Her tone was flat. "I smoke crack sometimes."

"Crack?" The conversation had gone wrong. "Where... how do you get crack?"

"The man down the street," she answered. "I do things for him." I knew what she meant.

We stared ahead. I swallowed the air's dusty heat.

The kid dashed back out. Beside her mother, she pointed in our direction. The woman nodded, and stepping toward us, the girl held out a Hershey bar. Over Mom's outstretched hand, I blurted, "She's not homeless. I have money. I can buy her one." Without thinking, I reached for my wallet to prove it. The child did what she was told, and as Mom smiled, the girl stepped to the side and left the chocolate on the wall.

"Are you crying?" Hope asked.

I wiped my eyes with the ball of my palm. "I'm not crying, Mom."

I went back the next morning and found Hope sitting on her bed. She pushed over to make room, and I held her hand tighter this time. "Will you let me tell them to move you?" I asked. "I can find a better place."

"No, I want to stay." She rested against the pillow, her eyes open. "Don't you need to go home, Andy?"

I kissed her hand. "I love you, Mom." I paused. I couldn't remember ever asking it, before or now. "Do you love me?"

She lifted her legs and rested her socked feet against my thigh. "Thank you, Andy. I'll see you later."

I left for home that afternoon.

The office number picked up. I introduced myself, mentioning that I had been there over the weekend. The woman answered she was aware of it, then changed her tone to tell me that she'd taken note of mine. I didn't ask for Pricilla to be moved—I ordered it. I was rude.

"Let me be as clear as possible. You run a slum. I want my mother moved out of there and away from you. Do you understand me?"

The woman said nothing at first. I rattled off my office number and asked her to repeat it. "Are you done, Mr. Bridge? She's only one patient. We'll get her moved."

While I thought to apologize and thank her, she hung up.

I knew it wasn't about the woman on the phone. It was about me. Mom's life wasn't going to get better. What it would do was get worse. With every year, a bit more of her was gone. When I finally did arrive, I had come too late.

Four days later, I got a call from the operator at another group home. Hope had been there for a day. When I asked if I could speak with her, the woman said she was resting. "Could you wake her up and get her to the phone?"

The stranger hesitated. "I don't think that's a good idea."

Unbeknownst to me, Hope had refused to leave her shed, even when the Maricopa County sheriff's deputies insisted. At five foot two and rail thin, Hope couldn't have put up much of a fight against the two men tasked with moving her.

Whatever had happened inside the shed, Hope left it handcuffed and screaming. She fell several times as the deputies dragged her across the dirt yard. By the time they got her to a patrol car, she had three cracked ribs, a broken wrist, and a swollen face. She was taken to the Maricopa County General Hospital, then escorted to her new group home that evening, her arm in a cast and her face packed with ice.

The deputies could've decided to stand down when Mom resisted being moved, or at the very least, they literally could have carried her to the patrol car instead of dragging her on the ground and letting her fall over and over. But I was the one who gave the order to change her placement, and I was also to blame for failing to realize that she might resist. Instead of abandoning the attempt to move Hope once it was clear that it couldn't be done gently—as any adequately trained mental health professional would've done—the manager called the deputies and told them to move her whether she cooperated or not. The manager was wrong. The deputies were wrong. But it was also my fault for trusting a system that I knew was broken.

When I finally reached Hope by phone, her voice was shockingly clear. "Andy, why did you do this?" I lied and said I didn't do it. I felt my eyes redden. She still had enough of a mother's instinct to tell her that her son was lying. That was the worst part: she knew it was my fault.

Chapter Eight

Three weeks after the Maricopa County sheriff's deputies moved Mom, I called Harvard's career office about jobs. The woman commented that the civil rights lawsuit in Alabama was famous. No, not just famous... it mattered.

A group of lawyers and mental health professionals founded the Bazelon Center for Mental Health Law in 1972. Since then, it had been a major force behind ending the savagery that was going on inside state institutions. Their work had helped establish a constitutional right for children with disabilities to receive "a free and appropriate public education." The Americans with Disabilities Act, or ADA, along with its protections against discrimination in employment, housing, transportation, daycare centers, hotels, movie theaters—whole swaths of public life—was due in large part to them. They had been involved in the *Wyatt* litigation from the start.

The woman hadn't exaggerated about the lawsuit.

Wyatt v. Stickney had begun in October of 1970, and it had dragged on for twenty-three years—most of my whole life. A federal court had ruled that every individual confined to a state mental institution had a constitutional right to treatment—specifically treatment that gave them a realistic opportunity of returning to society. As the court pointedly wrote, it wasn't only a constitutional right but a moral one as well. The decision was a turning point, a landmark ruling. But those governing Alabama didn't appreciate being told what to do by a federal judge, and they stuck to their position that patients in their institutions had no such right, constitutional or otherwise. What patients got, and how and when they got it, was the state's business alone.

The litigation had pushed through six American presidencies, and the defendants included a succession of Alabama governors. By the time I had sat down for my interview with the Bazelon Center's legal director, *Wyatt v. Stickney* had become the longest running, most bitterly fought mental health lawsuit in United States history.

Much of the 1970s were wasted answering Alabama's appeals on virtually every imaginable issue to avoid compliance. Then in January of 1980, the state shifted its position. Suddenly, it agreed to meet all the court's requirements within eighteen months, but that never happened. When the deadline passed, the state turned around and argued that what the federal court had done was unconstitutional after all. That change in tactics consumed the next five years. Exhausted, the parties hammered out a 1986 consent decree, under which Alabama promised to abide by the court's original orders. Money was set aside for improvements, and the bureaucracy clicked into place.

Slow as it was, change was finally happening.

Then without warning, the state again pulled the plug on the proposed reforms, claiming that its chain of public psychiatric hospitals had done enough. Taubman hadn't mentioned that on January 22, 1993, only weeks before we met, lawyers had already returned to court on behalf of the state's patients. Their argument was straight up: Alabama, in direct violation of the court's orders, had refused to offer patients the basic treatment that might allow them to leave an institution and gain something of a normal life. Instead, patients remained in state hospitals that were little more than filthy holding pens.

Eufaula, which opened its gates in 1972, was one of the last mental institutions that Alabama had built or, for that matter, would ever build again. Officials first chose the sinister-sounding name Eufaula Adjustment Center, which they changed to the more inviting Eufaula Adolescent Center a few years later. The facility was initially intended for 250 children who would otherwise have to live with the adult patients at Bryce Hospital.

Alabama announced, three years later, that it was doubling the size of the facility to five hundred children. Local officials put in their bid to acquire more land. The state anted up the construction costs, more than $4 million. "Do we support it?" Eufaula's mayor exclaimed, "Good gosh, yes, we do. It's important to our economy." Those five hundred children were bringing hundreds of new jobs with them.

Soon there were whispers of drug trafficking, sexual misconduct, abuse of children by staff, and an alarming lack of discipline.

"That place is not being managed right," the county sheriff had the courage to say. "I know for a fact that people are scared to talk." A Montgomery reporter went down to investigate, but he was barred from speaking with any children or staff, and the facility's director wasn't available to talk. "I'm the only one here," Eufaula's business manager claimed. After a frustrating meeting with the man, the reporter headed back to his motel, where someone flattened all four tires on his car. From the beginning, Eufaula was a pork-barrel project that the locals were going to protect.

Chapter Nine

More than a month after I had applied for the job, Jerry Taubman called. "If you would like the position, it's yours," he announced. "You'll need to be here by the first week in April. The position pays twenty-two thousand dollars a year." He reminded me not to expect to be there for more than two years, and that was if the case went to trial.

At around five o'clock, the firm's managing partner looked up from his desk and waved at me to sit. I hadn't practiced my opening lines and began rambling about not leaving for a competitor. I was going to a public-interest law firm in Washington, DC.

"That's a big change," he commented. "Leaving for Washington and a lawsuit in Alabama? Don't worry, we'll take you back."

I looked down at my polished loafers. I gave my three-week notice.

I stepped into the Bazelon Center's cramped lobby on April Fool's Day. The reception desk was empty. I took a seat on the single couch and waited almost an hour before a lanky middle-aged man with a goatee appeared and showed me to my new office.

"Your business cards should come in a week. I'm around the corner." I slid my briefcase under the worn, slick desk. "Oh, almost forgot." He smiled. "I'm Malcolm, your assistant."

The coming fight with Alabama would bring more lawyers, but for now, there were only four of us. There was Jerry, and then immediately under him were Brenda Artino and Jennifer Baxter. They were already too busy to spend time hand-holding a new junior lawyer. Getting up to speed was my job.

Without the faintest idea of where to start, I caught up with Brenda in the hallway and asked what I could do. "I don't know," she said, then pointed to a corridor lined with filing cabinets. "Read the case pleadings, I guess. You might want to start with Bryce Hospital. It's where it all got going." She shot me a look straight in the face. "Isn't your mom in a psych facility?"

"Yeah, she was," I answered quietly.

For two weeks, I piled armfuls of yellowed file folders on my desk. Smashed interrogatories and depositions, briefs and court orders, individual patient histories and lawyers' handwritten notes, all of it growing around me like stacks of old magazines in a dentist's office.

It all traced back to 1970, when Alabama cut its cigarette tax. To make up for the shortfall, the state sliced into funding for staffing and patient care at psychiatric facilities. Bryce Hospital was the oldest and largest institution in the state. Opened in 1861, it had started as a single brick building housing roughly fifty patients. By the time the court ruled in *Wyatt v. Stickney*, Bryce had swollen to a sprawling complex of wards confining more than five thousand men, women, and children.

"If a person stays here two weeks," as one administrator at Bryce put it, "he will probably stay a month, and if he stays a month, he will probably stay a year... and if he stays five years, he will probably stay a lifetime."

Alabama's budget cuts at Bryce were devastating. By the time staff terminations were finished, there was one nurse for every 240 patients, one physician for every 300, and one psychiatrist for every 1,670. Patients felt the brunt of it all, right down to the fifty cents a day allotted to feed them.

The state might have gotten away with it had they not laid off Mildred Rawlins. The nurse's aide was not just a terminated employee. She was also the great-aunt and legal guardian of seventeen-year-old Ricky Wyatt, who had been confined to the hospital two years before. Rawlins sued Alabama over the devastation of patient care. Those in charge struck back, cutting off all visits between Ricky and his family. Rawlins kept pushing. Appearing in Montgomery federal court, she demanded her job back and better conditions for her nephew—for all the patients at Bryce.

The dispute went to District Judge Frank Johnson—the same judge who would go on to hire Jerry as a law clerk not long after. Johnson heard out Rawlins's argument, then promptly told her that the state had the right to hire and fire employees as it chose and that no federal judge had any business trying to force Alabama to take back a terminated employee, even her. Rawlins's employment claim was dead on arrival.

But there was still that second complaint that she had brought on behalf of her nephew Ricky. That matter did fall within the authority of a federal judge to review, and so began the fight over what would happen to men, women, and children once they disappeared into Bryce's crowded wards.

Probate courts across Alabama had confined patients to Bryce with no hope of them ever getting out and, in so doing, denied them the basic constitutional protections that accused criminals take for granted. A shoplifter had his right to a lawyer, to confront those who testified against him, and to offer up his own defense. He got his day in court. Accuse someone of being mentally ill and all of that was gone. Although each of the thousands of patients locked inside Bryce were given a commitment hearing, they were brief and perfunctory affairs. They stood before a judge without a lawyer and were left to argue for their freedom as best they could. On paper, it looked like due process, but in practice it was a mere formality that could send them to Bryce for life.

Judge Johnson rightly concluded that Bryce Hospital had become little more than a penitentiary where one could be held indefinitely for no convicted offense. He ordered that involuntary hospitalization had to go beyond punishment or warehousing, ruling that involuntarily committed patients had a constitutional right to adequate treatment from a medical standpoint. And even if patients couldn't be cured, they had the right to the realistic opportunity of improving their mental condition and getting the chance to have a life outside an institution. No other judge had ever gone that far.

Johnson didn't trust the state to clean up Bryce at its own pace. In fact, he issued an ultimatum: correct the problems at Bryce Hospital *within six months* or he would appoint a panel of experts who would provide Alabama with basic standards for operating the facility. If conditions weren't improved, Johnson warned that he'd go beyond Bryce and include every other mental institution in the state. Full inspections would be conducted at each one of them, too.

Then came a surprise.

On Saturday morning, July 31, 1971, Alabama's newly appointed deputy commissioner for mental health woke to an early call. Dr. James Folsom listened while a distraught employee stammered through the line that the United States Attorney and a pack of reporters had arrived at Bryce's doorstep demanding to be let inside.

While reporters took notes and snapped photographs, Folsom ordered staff to unlock the wooden doors to the facility. What they found shocked them. Walking through the main building, the group discovered corridors crowded with beds and wood floors buckled from human feculence. Newspapers captured staff, including Folsom himself, scurrying to clean up what they could with mops and hoses.

It didn't take long for what reporters had seen to hit the news. The day after that unexpected Saturday morning visit, headlines splashed across the Sunday papers and on the days that followed.

The associate editor for the *Tuscaloosa News* described wards with "feces caked on toilets, patients who had not been bathed in days, urine on the floors, stopped up plumbing, beds without linen and generally deplorable conditions." Patients slept on floors, archaic shower stalls were cracked with spewing showerheads, and the inescapable stench hung everywhere. With ward temperatures reaching as high as 110 degrees, hospital officials admitted that patients had died from the heat. A number of residents lived in "barn-like structures" scattered across the grounds. Fire and other emergency hazards plagued the facility. With the images of Germany's World War II atrocities still fresh in mind, the editor of the *Montgomery Advertiser* labeled Bryce a "concentration camp."

One attorney commented on the wholesale use of tranquilizers: "You don't have to have locked doors and real fences if you're going to medicate patients into a stupor." Another who toured Bryce's grounds noted, "There was a cemetery in the back, but no records. Someone would die—they would merely dump them in an unmarked grave and that was the end of it and no accountability, supervision, no investigation to determine the cause of death—nothing." Bryce had become a chasm of destitution, which one observer suggested ought to be emptied of human beings, then submitted to "bulldozer therapy."

That Saturday morning at Bryce was only the beginning. The following week, attorneys and reporters arrived at the Partlow State School and Hospital, Alabama's institution for those with mental disabilities. Though not part of Rawlins's lawsuit against the state, conditions at Partlow were arguably worse. Visitors found groups of children in straitjackets, with other patients tied to chairs and urine-stained beds. Unable to brush away insects, restrained patients did nothing as flies crawled through their mouths. In one recreation yard, the tour discovered a single attendant left to watch more than eighty children "eating dirt and drinking water flowing off the wards." Entering the grounds, one attorney recalled, "The first thing I did was vomit. The whole place smelled like urine and sour milk." Staff opened a series of small rooms where bands of children deemed "too unruly" were locked up together. This time, Folsom chose not to show up.

Immediately after those visits, Judge Johnson added all of Alabama's other psychiatric institutions and developmental disability facilities to the lawsuit. The expansion couldn't have come as a surprise, because Johnson had warned Alabama he would do just that. Nine months had passed since the case was first filed, and as the press reports had shown, patients remained locked in squalor.

Working with outside experts and the state, Johnson announced that proper standards would be set for every psychiatric institution and developmental facility in the state—standards of care that would guarantee that patients' basic rights would be met and maintained. At the judge's request, President Richard Nixon's Department of Justice joined the lawsuit, and for the first time, the federal government was directly defending the rights of people committed to mental institutions. Johnson hadn't been bluffing, and Ricky Wyatt now represented nearly ten thousand people.

Frank Minis Johnson was thirty-seven when President Dwight Eisenhower appointed him to the federal district court. He took up his new post in 1955, one year after the Supreme Court reversed its defense of racial segregation in public schools. After Rosa Parks refused to give up her seat on a Montgomery bus, Johnson cast the deciding vote striking down his own city's segregated public transportation system. When the City of Tuskegee gerrymandered its voting districts to exclude Black voters, he ordered every voting precinct in Alabama to comply with the principle of "one man, one vote." And when hundreds of school districts defended their snail-paced integration plans, Johnson issued the country's first statewide desegregation order. Case by case, Judge Johnson undid Jim Crow across the state where he had lived his whole life.

But he had a price to pay. The Ku Klux Klan sat in his courtroom. The men left their white hoods at home. Johnson knew who they were by their faces. Montgomery's white community ostracized Johnson's wife and son; a cross was burned on his front lawn; his mother's house was bombed. Fanning the flames, Alabama's governor George Wallace called Johnson, with whom he had attended law school and had known for years, "a no-good goddamn lying son of a bitch race-mixing bastard" and yelled out to supporters at campaign stops that what the judge needed was "a barbed-wire enema."

When Johnson began his hearings to clean up Bryce Hospital and every other state institution in 1971, Alabama's own experts admitted that Bryce's conditions were beyond deficient. The lawyers defending the state agreed not to object. "The court is not wrong," they wrote Wallace, "and would be affirmed on appeal."

Confronted with that reality, Governor Wallace told his lawyers to cooperate in crafting the court's final ruling. The lawyers for both sides, along with mental hospital administrators and national experts, went to work on hammering out a set of standards that met the constitutional rights Johnson had carved out for people with mental illness.

The fact that Wallace had helped establish a set of constitutional rights for patients in mental institutions wouldn't sit well with his base. So he lied. Running for president on a promise to "Lead America to New Greatness," he shouted to his supporters at campaign rallies that he had nothing to do with any of it. Southern rights trumped whatever a judge had to say about state psychiatric institutions. The governor indignantly yelled that Frank Johnson was "tryin' to tell us down in Alabama how we can spend our own tax money." To cheering crowds in Pennsylvania and Texas he warned, "If he can do it to us, he can do it to you."

Wallace wasn't the only one who turned on Johnson. The newspapers that had shown up at Bryce in the first place and published what they had seen came out against him, too. In a succession of opinion pieces, the *Montgomery Advertiser*—the same editorial board that called Bryce a concentration camp—changed its tune. They claimed Johnson was "heavy-handed" and that his orders were unrealistic and naïve.

But none of that changed what Frank Johnson had done. He had set a legal precedent that stretched well beyond Alabama's borders. If Alabama's patients had rights under the constitution, then patients in any state could make the same argument. Lawsuits to protect the rights of adults and children in America's mental institutions sprung up in courts around the country, including in New York, New Jersey, Florida, Oklahoma, and Nebraska.

At the time of Johnson's ruling, Hope was at Camarillo State Mental Hospital, a short drive from Los Angeles up the coast. She was beginning the first of many involuntary confinements in psychiatric institutions. Thanks to Judge Johnson, the law now recognized that my mom and others like her had a right to privacy and dignity and to receive proper medical care. Johnson's decision gave her the right to be free from excessive medication. By law, she could not be medicated for the convenience of staff. Hospital officials could no longer force her to undergo experimental research or electric shock treatment. Without her or my consent, she could not be lobotomized.

Chapter Ten

Three weeks into my new job, the legal director called me into his office, where he and the two senior attorneys were crowded around his desk.

"We're talking about where to assign you," Jerry said. "We've divided the class members into sets and subsets, based on age and type of institution." He asked if I had a preference. He handed the other two my résumé.

I looked at the three of them and said, "Children."

"All right, children," Jerry answered, nodding at the others. "That gives him Eufaula."

"Makes sense," said Brenda, folding my résumé in half. "You can handle it." She'd be taking the adult mental institutions. Jennifer was put in charge of the other side of the lawsuit, the state's string of facilities that housed adults and children with developmental disabilities.

Jerry went through the basics we needed to get done and the hurdles that would come with them. Requests for the production of internal state documents were to be drafted. The state would object to the expense of copying and mailing them—the argument was a loser, but Alabama was sure to use it to draw out the process. As Jerry said it, his voice sounded concerned. We'd have to trust that the heads of each institution, and of course their bosses in Montgomery, would turn over *all* evidence. That included whatever was damaging to their own case. They were required to do it under court rules. Patients' records were vital. Every patient was our client, which allowed us to access their personal histories and treatment.

Our experts would have to comb through thousands of those records to establish their overall opinion of hospital care and treatment. Jerry had reached out to a number of people—most had worked for a state mental system or run a psychiatric institution. Those insights would be critical when they inspected Alabama's facilities—they'd know what to look for.

"They'll cut through the horseshit," Brenda joked.

Jerry paused before adding, "And they'll all have to be paid."

We would also be going to the facilities ourselves. If we got lucky, a few administrative staff might come forward to testify about what they'd seen. That was a stretch, Jennifer remarked. More likely, we'd have to depose them. The judge had told both sides to expect a trial date in the next twelve months.

Alabama's most effective weapon wasn't the facts or the law. Its true weapon was time—it always had been. Time meant money, and Alabama had plenty of both. Whether they liked or knew it, the state's taxpayers would pay for every phone call, lunch, and billable hour. We were left to individual donations and foundation grants, which could run out at any time.

Chapter Eleven

In stark contrast to the conditions at Bryce Hospital in the twentieth century, the institution that eventually bore Dr. Peter Bryce's name had been intended to be a model of compassion in its day. Alabama had hoped for a new beginning in treating mental illness.

The Alabama Insane Hospital opened its doors in 1861, the year the Civil War broke out. The building was "on a gentle elevation, surrounded by a farm and supplied with water from an unfailing spring." Attention was paid to light and air quality. Gas lighting offered security against fire, while ensuring that the halls were "cheerful and brilliant" at night and would lift the spirits of patients who were otherwise "disposed, by disease, to a depressed and gloomy state of mind." Planners ordered a brand-new Worthington steam pump from Brooklyn, New York, guaranteeing warmth in winter without "the suffocating quality of ordinary furnace heat."

With only fifty patients, accommodations were impressive. The rooms had views of the sweeping grounds. Every ward had a "distinct dining room, parlor, bathroom, drying room and water closet." Watercolor postcards celebrated its opening, depicting the long road that began at the hospital's gate, then cut through the abundant landscape planted with oak, magnolia, and pistachio trees before ending at the white-columned, dome-capped Italianate doors. This was the "moral architecture" that cared for body and mind.

Dr. Peter Bryce, the first superintendent, flat out banned bolts, bars, chains, manacles, and cages. In a dramatic break from accepted practice, no one would be chained to a wall or a bed, no one would be left walking spread-eagle with iron bars locked between their ankles, no one would be strapped into a straitjacket. However, nineteenth-century compassion had its limits—for example, Bryce did permit the use of "cross halls" that today are called "seclusion rooms."

But expectations for the new hospital were clear, and cruelty would never be tolerated. Attendants were to treat the patients with "uniform attention and respect," greeting them with kindness and goodwill. They were never "to address a patient coarsely or by nick-name." Every patient was to be "decently dressed for the day." Rooms, halls, and stairs were carefully swept and the floors, walls, and windows washed when required. Patients were "to be soothed and calmed when irritated; encouraged and cheered when melancholy and depressed." Above all else, they were never to be "pushed, collared, or rudely handled."

Although a few patients paid, most were young and poor farmers, their wives, and daughters. The institutionalization of children was rare but not unheard of. The most common causes of insanity were described as ill health, religious excitement, political excitement, epilepsy, and just plain bad habits. Other causes included jealousy and "disappointment in love." The practice was to lump people together—mental illness, mental disability, and even alcoholism were all treated the same way.

However, Peter Bryce remained a committed racist. From the start, the hospital had a small number of Black patients. Bryce admitted one of his own former slaves in 1867, a man whom the doctor had brought with him from South Carolina when he became superintendent. Shortly after that, Bryce admitted another recently emancipated slave, listing the "exciting" cause of the man's insanity as "freedom." Blacks were housed in the asylum's basement. However, as their number grew, officials ordered the construction of cheaper, segregated wards behind the main building.

When Bryce died in 1892 and the institution was renamed in his honor, the patient census had drastically multiplied from 50 to 1,258 men and women. As the tangle of wards grew, so did the need for patient labor to build and maintain them. With limited state funds and constant shortfalls, the hospital had always depended on patients working to offset operating costs. White females worked inside, helping nurses with housekeeping and sewing clothes for poorer patients. Black women—along with all men regardless of race—worked the outside grounds, which had grown to more than 1,100 acres within three decades. Watched by hired overseers, patients carved out roads and dug coal from an on-site mine. Patients grew crops, fired bricks, and built new wards to accommodate the increasing influx of new arrivals.

A facility dedicated to the humane treatment of the "insane" was considered revolutionary at the time, but relationships with physicians were hardly cordial. Patients sat mutely on small benches affixed to walls while physicians passed through the wards. Doctors were distant managers, touring each ward once every other day on "inspection" rounds at specified times. Ward nurses were the true disciplinarians, left in charge of daily patient treatment and supervision.

Caring for individuals with mental illness was usually a first job, and one that few kept for very long. Nurses were not the educated professionals found in today's hospital wards. They were untrained asylum attendants, part domestic servants and part frontline managers. Required to live among the patients themselves, male and female nurses were often in their teens. Years younger than the men and women whose lives they controlled, they weren't above playing favorites. Like their charges, nurses generally arrived at the hospital from the countryside with little or no education. Occasionally, discharged patients stayed on or returned as nurses. They were poorly paid and fined for a multitude of rule infractions, including loitering on errands, inattention to cleanliness—virtually any act not meeting a doctor's approval. Nurses were forced to remain on their wards from the "morning bell until bedtime" and only allowed to leave the hospital every other Sunday. It was a breeding ground for petty and vindictive behavior.

The first accounts of cruelty and abuse slipped into local newspapers at the turn of the last century. The 1907 summer was a dry one for cotton when Alabama's governor appointed a three-man commission to investigate the reports. Commissioners took testimony in Birmingham and Montgomery, and at Bryce itself.

Before the commission began its work, Alabama had already acquired the grounds of a former military arsenal in Mount Vernon that had incarcerated Geronimo and four hundred other Apache prisoners of war. Alabama chose the military arsenal to establish the state's segregated mental hospital for Blacks in 1900. The remote and isolated compound comprised a collection of slapped-together shacks rather than the hospital wards at Bryce. With only the most inexperienced doctors and staff consigned to it, the Mount Vernon Hospital for the Colored Insane lacked even the pretense of medical advancement awarded its companion white institution. In fact, the man for whom Mount Vernon was later renamed, Dr. James Searcy, remained at his post in Tuscaloosa as the new superintendent of Bryce, leaving the running of the facility for Black patients to his underlings.

The commissioners shared Dr. Searcy's racism. The year before they were appointed, dozens of Black patients had died of disease at Mount Vernon. Despite that, they had no interest in investigating that facility. They never traveled to Mount Vernon, requested records, or called a single witness from it.

What the commission heard about Bryce alone was brutal. A former Bryce nurse described patients working in gravel pits. In one altercation, a man had tried to escape while he was paving a hospital road. A group of nurses caught up with him about a half mile away, "threw him down in the road and kicked him considerably." The gang hauled him back to the road site and, in the airless summer heat, "made him trot with a wheelbarrow" and work twice as hard as anyone else. The man died.

A handyman described a visit to the male patients' wing: "Once while working on hall 13 I saw a [male nurse] ... take a man named Thompson, a patient, and throw him on the floor and step on his neck with one foot, throwing his whole weight on that foot ... I asked him what he meant by the like of that foot, and he said 'That is the way I control them.'" Mr. Thompson had been at Bryce for several years and was not, at the time, behaving in a "violent or wild" manner. Asked if Mr. Thompson begged for mercy, the handyman replied, "No, he did not have anything to say."

Another employee called out the consequences of speaking to a passing physician directly. A patient dared to approach the hospital's new superintendent, Dr. James Searcy. Once Dr. Searcy had moved on, a ward nurse kicked the patient repeatedly, striking him in his face and jaw until he "tore his mouth up." Asked how he had found work at Bryce in the first place, the ward nurse admitted that he was an ex-convict and had been sentenced to twenty-five years in the state's penitentiary before the governor pardoned him. Dr. Searcy was warned about the man's criminal history but hired him to supervise patients anyway. He made the man head nurse on the men's ward.

Witness after witness exposed young, untrained, and poorly supervised nurses, finding cruelty in the most mundane activities. One former nurse noted that, instead of serving patients separate items of food, staff preferred to mix everything into a single slop to be dished out onto patients' plates. The commission chair retorted that "dements" mixed their food anyway. Employees and patients reported the exploitation of personal hygiene, the deliberate dulling of razors, and the strapping of rolled towels around patients' necks and limbs to force them into tubs of freezing water, while enlisting other inmates to assist them. Dr. Searcy declined to attend the commission's proceedings on the advice of his counsel.

After a single week of testimony, the commission issued its report. Two patients' deaths were referred to the Tuscaloosa local grand jury. Investigating each death over a weekend, jurors found no reason to bring charges against the nurses involved. No new oversight for the state's asylums was ordered. No one was prosecuted. No one lost their job. Then it all ended. The report was shelved.

Meanwhile, probate judges in the state's sixty-seven counties continued granting requests from families, physicians, neighbors, and communities at large for someone to be put away.

There was one line from the commission's report that would haunt that institution and every other one in the state. And it was a warning. Bryce Hospital wasn't the revolutionary institution that Alabama had intended. By the turn of the twentieth century, the commission wrote that Bryce had already become nothing more than a "veritable dumping ground" for people who weren't wanted.

It would be another six decades before attention turned again to conditions inside the state's mental health facilities when, in 1971, seventeen-year-old Ricky Wyatt became a plaintiff in the class-action suit that bears his name.

Chapter Twelve

Brenda and I arrived at Bryce Hospital in Tuscaloosa at 8:00 a.m. sharp. The swelter of Alabama in July was already in the air. I had been on the job for about three months. We had sent out our first round of discovery requests; most involved trying to get a sense of what life inside Bryce was actually like. The physical safety of patients was the top concern. We wanted to know about the staff's use of restraints and seclusion rooms, the overmedication of patients, and the actual psychiatric treatment that Bryce offered.

But Bryce hadn't turned over a single patient's history explaining why they had been confined to the hospital and what was being done for them. Alabama stuck to the same line—it's gonna take time. It wasn't an outright refusal, but we were getting worried. In the meantime, we would inspect the place ourselves.

We waited outside the hospital with James Tucker, our local lead counsel, until the expert we were flying in from Raleigh arrived.

Lining up our experts hadn't been easy given our limited resources. Experts cost money, and Alabama had a lot more to spend on them than we did. And you couldn't just hire anyone with the requisite expertise—they had to be good. Evaluating the institutions required parsing through reams of internal state documents, calculating staffing ratios, and sifting through patient histories, then drafting reports we would file with the court. That alone would take hundreds of hours. Then months later, they could expect to be summoned to testify at trial and subject to withering cross-examinations. Their reports and opinions would be challenged. Their education and experience, their professional worth were all fair game. Mistaking one date for another in a patient's chart, a simple error in adding up the number of staff on a ward—these could be used to show that their expert opinions were useless.

About one thousand patients were on Bryce Hospital's wards, and each was our client. We had called several weeks ahead; visits were our only hope of speaking with them confidentially, one-on-one. Staff were known to listen in on calls to patients, record the conversations in their charts, and forward those transcripts to administrators in Montgomery, who handed them over to the state's lawyers. It was the first face-off with our opponents. They would be looking for an excuse to head into court and demand that we be barred from inspecting this or any other of the state's institutions again. Brenda said it was my chance to get my feet wet. I needed to get a sense of which staff to approach and who to avoid. I'd have to speak with patients, learn when to press and when to hold back.

Our expert was Marci White, who had grown up in Fayetteville, North Carolina. Both her parents were raised on "working farms"—small plots where families grew peanuts, corn, or strawberries, whatever was selling at the time and could also feed the cows and pigs. They were churchgoing Southern Baptists and had done well for themselves. Her mother was the first woman in the family to go past high school. She earned a certificate in bookkeeping and dictation from a local business college and kept the books for a family who owned a dress shop in town. "You don't give up on people and you expect that they'll do what's right," Mrs. White told her daughter.

Marci learned the same from her father. A beekeeper on the side, he made his living managing a local drugstore. When the first group of Black high school students sat down at the store's lunch counter for hamburgers and milkshakes, a panicked waitress ran to the back office, asking him what she should do. He answered calmly, "Take their orders and serve them like everyone else." Later, when white parishioners began whispering complaints about too many Black families participating in services, her father reminded the church's deacons how scripture taught that everyone came from the same God. Confronted with the man's quiet modesty, the congregation dropped the matter, performing all services with their fellow worshipers, regardless of race.

Marci's parents saved their money and put her through college and social work school. They saw to it that she didn't have to borrow for her education. She was now just entering her forties and running a state psychiatric facility in Raleigh—one for children with serious mental illnesses and histories of being violent or assaultive. Never give up on anyone, never give up on a kid, everyone deserves forgiveness and another chance—Marci believed that. She got it from her parents.

We drove down the hospital's central road that cut through the 1,100-acre property and ended at the front doors. Centered in front of the hospital, a statue's uplifted arm trickled water into a flaking, aqua-painted pool. Here stood golden Hebe, goddess of forgiveness, offering wine and ambrosia to the gods. She faced the drive, greeting patients as they arrived. Once a patient passed and entered the hospital's doors, the goddess of forgiveness turned her back on them.

Alabama's legal team arrived, consisting of Tom Bass, the state's assistant attorney general, three state employees, and two attorneys hired from a local private firm. Once inside the main hospital building, Bass and his hired counsel immediately took the lead. We followed them up a grand oak staircase to the second floor and were told to take a seat outside what appeared to be a line of administrators' offices. There we sat and waited. After nearly an hour, Brenda got up and knocked on the closest door. I listened to her arguing with someone. Her voice sounded tense. She sat back down and threw a grimace at the rest of us. The delaying tactics had begun.

Bass reappeared. "We're thinking that y'all ought to meet the folks that run the hospital." Another hour passed while we were led through the rat's nest of offices, where we quietly listened to senior employees recite job descriptions, down to the last ledger entry and cleaning schedule. All refused to answer questions, stiffly informing us that the state's attorneys were to handle that. From there, we toured two of the hospital's cafeterias, were shown every kitchen. An administrator tapped on a brand-new dishwasher, announced that it had just been installed, and recited the rinse-cycle temperatures. We paced through the main performance auditorium, where we were told coed movie nights were scheduled every Friday, along with Sunday church services. A widening squad of employees gathered around us, trying to catch what bits of conversation they could.

When one of the two private attorneys for the state announced that new flowers had been planted across the outside grounds—if he remembered right, Alabama azaleas—James Tucker intervened from behind us. "That's not going to work," he said, shaking his head. "We'd like to see the long-term care units." He punctuated his request with a look at his wristwatch. An administrator grudgingly escorted us to the scramble of the hospital's oldest wards.

The pack of us moved on to the so-called back wards, a warren of private slums, where hundreds of human beings were consigned. The earliest accounts of life at Bryce Hospital described these chaotic units—most built by patients decades ago—as the corridors where the most violent or least responsive patients were held. Patients who offended a nurse or doctor, or were guilty of simply being disliked, could also find themselves dispatched here for months or even years. Selective ward assignment was an effective tool for punishment and control. Entering this, the largest of the wards we had toured, I expected noise, not the pin-dropping quiet that I found. Bryce was packed with life and, at the same time, empty of it.

"None of those work," an older male ward nurse yelled over to me, watching as I bent over the crusted water fountain. We had passed dozens of ward staff, but he was the first to volunteer anything to me, the first to speak to any of us. He waved his hand at an older patient. The woman shuffled toward the other women slumped on sagging sofas and recliners, most gazing in stupors at the small TV set to mute, others staring into the sun through the three high windows. Around us, an effluvium of vinegar-scented cleaning fluid drifted over sweating, unwashed bodies.

"Water intoxication," the ward nurse added dryly. He glanced up at the dangle of mismatched fluorescent lights. "Psychogenic polydipsia, turn your back, and they'll drink a gallon of it in an hour." Gulping it down, over and over, patients flooded their bloodstreams with water, turning the basis of life into poison. Individual cells swelled like balloons. The brain expanded, pressing against its skull and compressing its stem, until the patient fell into seizures, a coma, or died.

"I'm sorry, sir. They?" I hesitated in front of him.

"The schizophrenics, but some of the others, too. Admin had those faucets shut off since before I got here, ten years ago. Gets hot here in the summer."

"Is there a fountain working anywhere? I could also use a restroom." I turned toward the corridor covered in pale yellow paint, blocked by oversize white wooden doors opening into congregate sleeping units.

"Staff bathrooms are around the corner," he said, throwing a nod over my shoulder. Next to the recreation room, I spoke up finally, introducing myself to the older woman. I extended my hand. "What's your name, ma'am? I'm Andrew." Halting in front of me, half-clothed in a threadbare pink hospital gown, she pulled her thumb from her mouth, dropping her saliva-covered hand into mine.

Her head tremored, her mouth slacked open, and I caught the sharp sweet smell of her breath. "Are you my grandson?" she asked.

"No, ma'am." I paused, caught in her withered eyes. "I'm sorry, I'm not your grandson." As I released her hand, she hung next to me. I gazed down at the cracked marbled flooring. "Were you wanting to watch some TV?" I asked, trying to keep the conversation going.

A third of the way down the corridor, Bass paced up. "Do that again and this tour y'all got going here gets shut down. You got that, Andrew?" he barked, his voice pounding down the ward. Dozens of patients turned. So did the touring group. Brenda broke away from our expert and wedged herself between the older woman and me, inches from the man's face.

"Listen up, Tom," she snapped. "This patient happens to be a client of ours. Mr. Bridge can talk to whoever he wants to."

In an apparent routine between the two of them, he snarled back, "Not if he's disturbful of the institution's therapeutic milieu."

My colleague jabbed her finger at him. "The only one disturbing the *therapeutic milieu,* as you call it, is you, Tom, for violating the federal court order that gives Mr. Bridge, our expert, me, and our local counsel the right to speak to anyone—patients, *that* employee, and whoever else you've got here—when, where, and how we please."

With a sidelong look at Brenda, then me, he countered with a promise: "You just keep on doing it, 'cause y'all ain't winning this time."

A short step from the assembled hospital administrators, Bass halted. "Andrew," he yelled back, grinning, "my colleague tells me that old woman next to you with the drool on her hand has hepatitis."

I knew better than to respond.

Rounding the corner into an empty corridor, I pushed through the first door into a room where moss-colored tiles stopped several feet from the ceiling. A dust-covered collection of salon-style hair dryers were crowded opposite a row of men's barber chairs. Stacked to the side were plastic trays of brushes and cheerfully colored rollers. An intimacy of anonymous lives filled the space. I thought of Hope, who had supported us as a hairdresser when she was well. And I imagined a woman having her hair done, as close to how she liked it before she was sent here.

But I was wrong. This was not a salon, at least not originally. A swinging door adjoined the room and beside it, a narrow observation pane cut through the wall above a network of rusting pipes. I stared at the overhead monitor that watchful staff had used to mind heart rates and other vitals of the patient lying on the operating table in front of them. In this place, tiled in identical mossy green, intimacy gave way to excruciating violation. This was where patient psychosurgeries were performed.

The earliest endeavors at psychosurgery were performed on people with schizophrenia, all inmates at a Swiss asylum on the shores of Lake Neuchâtel in 1888. The asylum's director, Dr. Gottlieb Burckhardt, wasn't satisfied with the accepted practice that limited surgery to human autopsies and live dogs. Burckhardt took things a step further and began cutting open the skulls of his patients who couldn't tell him no.

The first patient was a thirty-one-year-old lithographer. Burckhardt, who had no surgical training, removed pieces of the man's frontal cortex with "a sharp spoon." He reported that the man was calmer and more conversational, though he developed seizures. Despite that alarming result, he went on to perform the "procedure" on another five patients. He offered his results to the 1899 Berlin Medical Congress, where his presentation "caused a chill in the room." From the start, lobotomizing a human being had its detractors.

Several decades later, Portuguese neurologist António Egas Moniz inserted a small surgical rod with a retractable wire loop into a patient's brain. Moniz's plunger-activated instrument went through the cortex, then cored out the nerve tract behind it. Moniz and his partner operated on twenty individuals between November 1935 and February 1936. Their records were spotty, and they were poor at follow-ups. But unlike Burckhardt, Moniz promoted his work across Europe. The prefrontal lobotomy was born, a development for which Moniz later won the Nobel Prize.

Yet nothing could beat an American showman. Young and ambitious, Dr. Walter Freeman wanted to make a name for himself. He found his fame in the squalor of psychiatric wards. Freeman performed the first lobotomy in the United States on September 14, 1936, on a Kansas woman named Alice Hood Hammatt. According to her case history, Alice was "high strung, emotional and easily fatigued, a meticulous housekeeper with several previous breakdowns." In surgery that took an hour, Freeman and his partner Dr. James Watts took twelve cores from Alice's brain. The *Washington Evening Star* reporter who was invited to watch Alice's lobotomy quoted her conversation with Freeman the following day:

Doctor: "Do you have any of your old fears?"

Alice: "No."

Doctor: "What were you afraid of?"

Alice: "I don't know. I seem to forget."

Doctor: "Do you remember being upset when you came here?"

Alice: "Yes, I was quite upset, wasn't I?"

Doctor: "What was it all about?"

Alice: "I don't know. I seem to have forgotten. It doesn't seem important now."

Under the front-page banner BRAIN OPERATION BY DC DOCTORS AIDS MENTAL ILLS, the reporter concluded that what Freeman and Watts had done with Hammatt and five subsequent patients "probably constitutes one of the greatest surgical innovations of this generation." Freeman apparently agreed. "It seemed unbelievable that uncontrollable sorrow," he remarked, "could be changed into normal resignation with an auger and a knife."

As Freeman's lobotomies increased, so did his celebrity.

The existing prefrontal procedure was too expensive to be a practical option for the thousands of institutionalized men and women in America's psychiatric hospitals. Freeman needed something quicker and easier for widespread use. He came up with the idea of simplifying the lobotomy by pushing an ice pick through the eye socket. His son described his father's technique: "The first ice pick came right out of our kitchen drawer and it worked like a charm."

Without telling his partner, Freeman performed ice-pick lobotomies without sterile equipment or general anesthesia. He was in the middle of his tenth such procedure when Watts surprised him in his office. According to one account, "Watts entered an office and discovered Freeman standing over an unconscious patient who had an ice pick lodged in his orbit. Freeman asked his partner to assist him while he took a photograph." Watts walked out and never worked with Freeman again.

Freeman went on searching for subject patients confined to psychiatric hospitals. He contended that his "transorbital lobotomy" resulted in no meaningful intellectual or personality impairment and that it was a minor operation. On a decade-long barnstorm, he traveled the country on "head hunting expeditions," teaching poorly trained psychiatric hospital doctors how to conduct the procedure, while continuing to do it himself. "It takes about 10 minutes," he said. His ice pick was a quick and affordable means to resolve difficult patients and drain overcrowded wards. He recommended lobotomizing patients for irritating behavior, over-grieving, promiscuity, even pain from cancer.

"I believe this operation should be employed more frequently in patients with severe pain," he urged, adding that "the odd thing is that the physical part of the pain is never abolished by the operation. But in all cases the patients no longer mind the pain. Where they had said they could not endure pain any longer, after the operation the same people laughed at the pain and said it was nothing to worry about."

There were objections.

Freeman pressed the Veterans Administration to lobotomize soldiers returning from World War II who were having difficulty adjusting to civilian life. A "mass lobotomy" was proposed for the Tuskegee Veterans Administration Hospital in Alabama, a segregated facility for Black soldiers, but the national neurosurgeon consultant to the VA remarked that doctors would perform the procedure at the nation's VA hospitals "over [his] dead body." The assembly-line Tuskegee lobotomies never went forward, but the Veterans Administration chief psychiatrist left it to individual hospitals to decide if their psychiatrists could perform Freeman's transorbital lobotomies. That bureaucratic loophole allowed VA hospitals to lobotomize nearly 1,500 soldiers in less than five years after the end of World War II.

With the media gushing with glowing reviews, public support grew for the barbaric procedure. *Newsweek* magazine reported that "the operation had made mental patients... much easier to care for in the institutions." Another article advised that the operation was so simple that it "may help to clear the 'back' wards of our mental hospitals." During the heyday of the procedure, between forty and fifty thousand Americans were lobotomized.

Freeman's ice pick was finally replaced in 1954 by psychopharmacology with the arrival of Thorazine. Once given the drug, patients developed an "apparent indifference" to external stimuli. They became emotionally neutral. Thorazine's manufacturer went on a road show touring public mental institutions, where staff reported wards that suddenly went somnolent and quiet once the drug was administered. From Clarks Summit State Hospital in Pennsylvania to Lincoln State Hospital in Nebraska to Longview State Hospital in Cincinnati, the drug's reception was overwhelmingly positive. The more docile patient population made work easier for hospital staff.

Thorazine produced no real dependency, though other side effects were becoming clear. Researchers reported patients' decreased mobility, reduced facial expressions, loss of initiative, and muscular rigidity, oddly similar to symptoms of Parkinson's disease. Patients also drooled and tended to fidget, walk in place, or repeatedly cross and uncross their legs. Underlying psychotic symptoms persisted, but now they were masked.

Available in tablets, syrups, suppositories, and by injection, the drug swept through already understaffed hospital wards. Within eight months of its introduction, Thorazine was being administered to two million patients.

The side effects of Thorazine became clearer and more pronounced. I saw them firsthand with my mother. Like every other new patient, she was given that drug to manage her behavior at her first psychiatric admission to Camarillo State Mental Hospital. Keeping with hospital drug routines, her behavior was regularly "maintained" at Camarillo with a shot of Thorazine along with the other drugs that began with her admission.

For Hope and other patients, Thorazine's consequences took time. Repeated, unmonitored doses produced tardive dyskinesia, the irreversible tics that caused Hope to smack her tongue inside her mouth, the grimaces that repeatedly swept across her face, the rigid movements of her arms and neck, and the fixed upward gaze in her eyes that made me think she was staring into the sun. There was the way she walked, her stiff legs dragging her feet behind her, later called the "Thorazine shuffle." They had all taken years to develop. Untold numbers of adults and children continued to be given Thorazine before its devastating consequences were understood.

Chapter Thirteen

What we found at Bryce was appalling. Brenda cornered one of the frontline orderlies in a patient dayroom. The man admitted that he and others "unofficially" secluded patients to get them out of their hair. That was only a start. Moving from staff to staff, she peppered them with questions: How were ward disturbances handled? How were medications evaluated? Why did some rooms smell like urine? Few were answered, but what we learned during that visit and others was enough.

There was evidence of skin tears, bruises, and gashes. There were broken bones and patient deaths. A twenty-six-old man, Norman L., had been admitted with a diagnosis of schizoaffective disorder. Norman died after being given excessive doses of antipsychotic medications. Another had lost a leg with what had started as an untreated gangrenous toe. Relentless use of antipsychotics with no psychiatric benefit served to subdue and sedate in place of actual treatment.

Alabama had opposed patients' right to privacy and dignity, going so far as demanding that the court eliminate it. The court had refused to revoke that right, but what was clear was that the state still refused to honor it. Adults stood naked in hallways while they waited for ward showers. Men and women sat draped in sheets while they ate. Where staff assisted with meals, they sat wordlessly stuffing food in patients' mouths. Patients in four-point restraints lying on rolling beds in the middle of hallways, spread-eagle with their wrists and hands tied to each corner. Older adults were the most vulnerable. Positioned in recliners and hospital chairs, they lined the walls of dayrooms on multiple wards. Dressed in nothing more than nightgowns and slippers, they spent hours shackled in place with crotch belts and vest restraints.

The patients at Bryce said it for themselves. Reflecting on her care at the hospital, one young woman observed, "I feel as though I was emotionally battered." An older gentleman appeared frightened when he muttered, "They treat you like a dog... and threaten to take away our privileges." Left forgotten in Bryce's admissions unit for eight months, another patient explained staff expectations: "They want us to sit like statues and act like robots."

Mom was admitted to Camarillo State Mental Hospital in 1969. When she arrived, Camarillo housed a mix of adults, children, and adolescents with mental illness, developmental disorders, drug and alcohol addiction, and dementia. As many as ninety-two patients occupied the female unit at a time, bed to bed packed together much like Bryce. As a patient who looked to be in otherwise good health upon her admission, Hope was given the usual antipsychotic cocktail for an individual with schizophrenia: 100 mg Thorazine, 5 mg Stelazine, and one-tenth of a grain of hyoscine. One shot knocked out the most acutely active patient in sixty to ninety minutes, keeping the quiet on Camarillo's wards, as they did at Bryce.

Mom had been committed to at least three psychiatric hospitals. Her first and longest confinement said a lot. Camarillo was touted as the largest psychiatric institution in the world, capable of housing between six to eight thousand patients at any given time. Throughout her twenties and into her early thirties, Hope was one of those patients. The Spanish-styled compound stretched across 1,600 acres of old ranchland. Not far from the Pacific Coast Highway, the institution was once rumored to be the inspiration behind the Eagles song "Hotel California." Perhaps it was the lyrics about a place where once admitted, one could never leave. The album cover resembled the Camarillo's bell tower, but it was in fact a grainy photo of the Beverly Hills Hotel. The song was a chart-topper in 1977, the same year the Ventura grand jury investigated conditions inside the notorious compound.

The members of the grand jury were offended by what they found. Drugs were indiscriminately prescribed and, at times, were forced on patients as a punishment. Violent altercations involving patients were poorly documented. Staff recorded incidents that had never happened. Other incidents were never reported, or if they were documented, they went ignored. Staff explanations for the use of cuff and belt restraints on patients were evasive. Many had crossed the line "into the territory of gross and criminal behavior."

The jurors wrote that employees who failed to meet acceptable medical standards needed to be fired. They demanded a change in hospital leadership. New practice manuals, certifications, and retraining—that all needed to be done. But at its core, Camarillo needed to change its lack of compassion. There was a coldness in the way staff spoke to patients, a mechanical manner in how they bathed and fed them, and a contempt for patients' concerns. Camarillo's physicians, frontline nurses, and orderlies needed to respect the lives of the men, women, and children they completely controlled.

The jury demanded "an active, vigorous public enlightenment program about this hospital, who it serves, and what it does." The group suggested that a good start would be to unlock the compound for regular open houses. They wanted the public to know what was going on inside Camarillo's quiet grounds. Because once people knew, the volunteers reasoned, they would also have to care.

I was starting high school, grinding my way through geometry and humming that Eagles tune. Mom was at Camarillo, and during her confinement, more than one hundred patients died there. Homicides weren't part of the grand jury's review. That responsibility went to the district attorney's office, and while the jurors were wrapping up their report, the local prosecutor announced that seventy-nine of those deaths were under criminal investigation.

Chapter Fourteen

In the steaming summer heat, James Tucker and I drove a good forty-five minutes down the rambling dirt road after splitting from the state highway. We hadn't had much time to talk during our first tour of Bryce. He was distracted navigating the road, but what I managed to get out of him was that he was married with two daughters. His legal career began at Florida Rural Legal Services, where he represented Lee County prisoners with AIDS, suing to stop jailers from following them around spraying clouds of disinfectant. As our local counsel, James knew Bryce well. He also knew where to find Ricky Wyatt, the lawsuit's first plaintiff.

We pulled up in front of a collection of broken house trailers with wooden add-ons, plastic-covered lean-tos, and rusting trucks. Catching a waft of chopped wood and garbage, I glanced at the encampment's most tended feature: a vegetable garden occupying roughly a third of the cleared land. The plot wasn't a pastime, it was a crop—something to live on. Planted in red iron mud, the garden pushed against the encroaching forest. The only other green was a pack of feral dogs covered in mossy mange. A small black mutt ran to my leg snarling up at me.

Alabama's backwoods were dotted with plots like this one. A mix of families, friends, and children squatted, living on what they could grow or trade. As for what couldn't be grown or traded, the inhabitants combined their disability and public assistance, or as James put it, "pooled the check" to gain what required actual cash: kitchen appliances, shoes, light bulbs, and rolling tobacco.

He pointed to an older woman sitting beside a firepit made of rocks torn from the surrounding mud. "That's Ricky's mom, Sylvia Wyatt."

She wore a black knitted cap, exposing her full face with milky blue eyes.

"Sylvia, this is Andrew Bridge," James began. "He's here to see you and your son." I held her age-spotted hand. "I'm glad to meet you, Mr. Bridge." James and I took our seats on a set of wobbly chairs. "It's good to meet you, Mrs. Wyatt."

Sylvia's father was an alcoholic, and on the day he died, his accumulated stints in county jails and Alabama penitentiaries totaled fifty-two years, making elementary school the longest single period he had not been incarcerated.

"My whole family background was a disaster." Sylvia bobbed her head at me. "My daddy belonged to the Klan, down in Southside down around Rosedale. He drank. By God, I never seen anyone drink like that. They'd start out by drinking the high-class stuff down by the old river bridge."

Sylvia grew up in one of Tuscaloosa's whites-only Jim Crow slums.

"By the next day, they got down to the shoe polish. You know, the little can? They'd melt it down and strain it through bread. They'd get to drinking Sterno, and his mouth'd turn red. Daddy'd get arrested and be in court the next day. The judge woulda spent the weekend with 'em and been just as drunk. Looking down from his bench, he'd ask, 'Well, where did you get the whiskey, Tommy?' And Daddy'd answer, 'Oh hell, Henry, you know where we got the whiskey.'"

"We're here about Bryce and the lawsuit," James interjected.

Sylvia tapped my leg over the cold firepit. "They gave good jobs there, good money."

Her grandfather worked the grounds at Bryce, and he took her along with him during school breaks. Left to her own devices, she used to wander around the property's cemetery where Bryce buried its patients. Every grave was marked with an anonymous iron stake.

She was sixteen when she had Ricky, and when James asked, she couldn't recall why the state took him from her.

"Here's my boy, Ricky." Sylvia pointed. "You know, Mr. Bridge, that lawsuit is named for him." James and I watched as a middle-aged man hobbled toward us across the dirt, cane in hand, pursued by the second pack of dogs emerging from a hoard of scrap metal and lawnmowers.

"It's good to meet you, Mr. Wyatt," I said.

He smiled and took a seat beside his mother. Ricky was now fifty-three years old.

Ricky was eleven when the state took him into custody. He was thirteen when Alabama officials told him he was leaving the Alabama Industrial School outside Birmingham. He had his choice: the Methodist Children's Home in Selma or the Sheriffs Youth Ranch in Marion. His aunt Mildred, a nurse's aide at Bryce Hospital, told him to go with the Methodist Children's Home. They'd look after him and offer better care, she promised. His aunt got it right. Ricky liked the staff, earned a weekly allowance, and made field trips into town. Things were good, at first.

But in two and a half years, the boy had only two family visits, both from Mildred. He had heard nothing from his mother, Sylvia. The boy was lonely. By his mid-teens, he was fighting, smoking, and defiant at school. A final outburst of anger changed everything.

"I was already behind, and the teacher asked me why I ain't done my homework." Ricky looked over at his mother, as if searching for her approval. "The teacher wanted to send me to the office. I just got up and turned my desk over. I said, 'I'll go,' and she yelled back, 'Well, I'll take ya.'"

A state probation officer woke Ricky the next morning in his bedroom. A car was waiting outside. Allowing the teenager to dress but pack nothing, the officer drove Ricky to Tuscaloosa County, which had kept jurisdiction over his case. Handcuffed inside the sheriff's office, Ricky looked up at the probation officer. "What are they gonna do with me now?" The officer pointed at the courthouse down the street. "I guess it's up to your aunt Mildred and the probate judge. I'm betting she's not taking you on that nurse's salary."

Inside the cramped courtroom, the judge listened as officials ticked off a list of offenses before concluding the teenager was a juvenile delinquent. The judge never requested to see Ricky, who was waiting less than a block away. The proceeding carried on despite the absence of a lawyer to represent the boy. Mildred was never called, nor was Sylvia or any other member of Ricky's family.

It wasn't hard to send someone away to Bryce. It began with a stop at the local courthouse. A frustrated husband, an envious neighbor, or a slighted boss could ask for a spot on the probate judge's calendar. The hearing was brief, about the length of a contested traffic ticket. A physician's signature and two witnesses were enough to get the person incarcerated in one of the psychiatric wards. The accused had no right to counsel or to a jury of his peers. The probate judge determined if the individual's accusers had offered satisfactory proof, and from that, he alone settled the matter, declaring the man, woman, or child sane or not. There was no appeal process.

Bryce Hospital's former director of patient advocacy admitted that while working at the institution, she had seen families commit indigent relatives for financial reasons and one teenage girl because she was involved with a Black man. In the absence of the required signatures and witnesses, copies of old commitment papers could be simply copied and reused. Failing that, a former Bryce Hospital employee cited a local judge who'd decided that a veterinarian's signature was good enough for a commitment.

"Anybody who was unwanted was put in Bryce," one Montgomery judge remarked. "They had a geriatric ward where people like your parents and grandparents were just warehoused because their children did not care to take care of them in the outside world, and probate judges would admit them and commit them to Bryce on a phone call, on a letter from a physician saying they could not take care of themselves. They were not mentally ill. There was one ward with nothing on it but old people. Beds were touching one another and they were simply warehoused."

By 1967, the chief physician for Alabama's mental institutions complained about the number of new patients being committed to Bryce each week. The shortage of registered nurses and other attending personnel was staggering. Wards were overcrowded and dilapidated. Bryce lacked the most basic capacity to accommodate the onslaught of 1,200 newly admitted patients in a single year. At most, it could provide some kind of care for a third of that number. The state did nothing. Probate judges continued to commit new asylum inmates across Alabama's sixty-seven counties, in perfunctory proceedings that took minutes.

While Ricky Wyatt waited in that probation office, new patients were arriving in the back of a county sheriff's car, confinement orders in hand. New arrivals were put through a degrading admission procedure that was like entering a prison. They were stripped of their clothing, deprived of personal belongings, assigned compulsory unpaid work, and denied any privacy, including private toilets. As one observer put it, they had arrived at the "crazy house."

Ricky's Tuscaloosa hearing lasted about twenty minutes. No one claimed that the boy was mentally ill or asked for a psychiatric evaluation. State officials got to the point: a stint at the mental hospital would teach the kid a lesson and get him back in line. That was enough. The judge ordered Ricky committed to Bryce Hospital, whose gates were ten minutes away. Just as the judge didn't care that the teenager wasn't mentally ill, he didn't care that Bryce had no children's unit to house him. The boy would be placed in one of the men's wards.

Bryce was a ramshackle firetrap with as many as sixty adults packed in a ward. Poorly supervised patients could be violent or sexually assaultive. Children saw that violence between adult patients and also were victims of it. Proper schooling was an impossibility. Educational progress halted, and children regressed. Staff had no special training in treating children and restrained them as they did adults with straitjackets and by locking them in seclusion cells "large enough for one bed and a coffee can that served as a toilet." The result was the opposite of effective treatment: children's mental health worsened, often showing signs of paranoia and psychosis.

Sylvia interrupted, "Ricky don't remember me visiting him, but I did. Nurses got him showered and dressed him in new clothes. He'd mostly sit there, staring at the floor."

Ricky signed an affidavit to the federal court that he had slept on wet floors and was being locked in a "cell-like room." That was when administrators struck back at the boy and his mother, immediately halting all visits between them.

"Before the sun was down, I was there, in Bryce Hospital. They said it was the best they could do." Ricky kicked at the firepit's edge. "I think they just got tired of me."

Chapter Fifteen

Only months before Ricky was sent to Bryce, Alabama considered creating a separate institution for children. Officials debated acquiring an abandoned radar base on the outskirts of the City of Eufaula for that purpose, then put off the idea for lack of money. But when confronted with negative publicity about Bryce, the Justice Department's intervention, and the unrelenting litigation, Alabama found the cash. Like MacLaren, the property came with hundreds of beds and was bought on the cheap. The initial plan was to house as many as 500 adolescents at Eufaula transferred from Bryce Hospital or admitted by their parents, but downsizing brought the number to 120. Since then, Eufaula had remained the state's largest psychiatric facility for children.

Jerry and Brenda assigned me the job of visiting the facility and told me to be on the lookout for frontline staff. They were the ones who had the most direct contact with the children. They read their charts, saw how social workers, psychologists, and psychiatrists interacted with them, and most importantly, they'd know if a child had ever been hurt at the facility. Providing us with that information could lead to more discoveries. If a member of staff agreed to go further and testify at trial or cooperate under oath in a deposition, their words could be damning. However, none of the administrators, treatment staff, or ward workers ever came forward.

Children had never been a focus of the lawsuit. But what had happened to those two boys—David Dolihite, who had survived a suicide attempt, and Eddie Weidinger, who hadn't—opened Eufaula to investigation in a way that it had never been. I was to get a good look at the facility, but my real goal was to interview the children or, as Eufaula called them, "residents."

When David was admitted on January 13, 1992, at the age of fifteen, he had no history of alcohol or drug abuse. Ten days after his arrival, David's fully assembled psychological team signed his master treatment plan. According to the staff's assessment, David was now describing "prior suicide attempts, gestures, and was known to have frequent suicidal ideations." His medical records noted his grandmother committed suicide, and he had written a poem to his girlfriend a year earlier that described his own death. A Eufaula psychologist wrote that the teenager was now reporting feeling suicidal when he got angry and having trouble sleeping. David's treatment plan said, among other things, that he was suffering an active suicidal ideation and gesture problem. However, a clinical team member noted that the Dolihite family had no knowledge of any prior suicide attempts by David and that his self-reported past gestures could not be confirmed. Locked away and forbidden to speak with his family, David began to veer downward—rapidly.

David hurt himself for the first time three days after Eufaula's staff had finished up their evaluation of him. He stabbed his left wrist. No one reported how he'd done it, but the puncture wound was deep, and he told the Eufaula nurse that he "was going to cut his arm off and kill himself." Staff placed him on one-on-one observation. The following day, a Eufaula social worker completed a suicide assessment but concluded that David's suicidal thoughts were intermittent and without genuine intent. Perhaps. But that did nothing to explain why he was threatening himself, and why staff did nothing to help him.

On at least two occasions, medical records indicated that despite being aware of David's need for intense therapy, his social worker failed to appear for his individual sessions. "Because of time constraints," the case said. Alleged to have used time-out and restraint methods as punishment and not as therapy, David's social worker had been reprimanded for demeaning a child. She also was alleged to have known of the abuse being inflicted on children but appeared not to care. Worse, she was reported to have engaged in abusive behavior herself.

According to children's affidavits as well as frontline staff member Allen Forte, there was gang violence between residents at Eufaula, as well as abuse by staff. One boy reported that David had run into his ward room to hide from gang members, that he had told David's social worker that gangs were threatening David, and that staff were allowing gangs to mistreat other children. The child went on to say that he had seen staff hit David and another resident numerous times. The boy was brave enough to report it to Eufaula's director, a Eufaula psychologist, and David's social worker. Forte backed the boy up, testifying that he had seen supervisors strike children, that active gangs had assaulted children, and that one twelve-year-old child had been sexually abused twice by other residents. The child had to be taken to the hospital both times for injuries incurred during each assault.

Eufaula's director clearly knew of reported assaults by staff and children, as well as sexual abuse. Yet he took no steps to end it and failed to open a professional investigation. He was also aware of the inappropriate seclusion of children.

David had to be desperately frightened.

The week after David hurt himself for the first time, he cut his left wrist again. Shortly after that, a staff member reported that he wrote with a rock on the security screen over his ward room window, "Oh, God I want to die, please take me or I'll commit suicide, Death, Suicide are the facts of life." Staff put him on work restitution for damaging the security screen and restricted him to his ward for two days. Typically, David would've been required to mop up floors or clean the boys' showers. However, Eufaula's staff also used a bizarre and abusive tactic to deal with children who hurt themselves: they were required to do push-ups in front of staff. The rule was ten for every cut and could add up literally into hundreds for a single child. But after David hurt himself again, no second suicide assessment was completed, no additional therapeutic interventions were undertaken, and no psychiatrist or psychologist visited him regarding the incident. The next day, staff secluded him for being a "threat to the community group." No one called David's parents.

David's parents could've told them their son's history, what reassured him, what scared him, and what he wanted. Closed-off evaluations of institutionalized children had limited reliability without considering what the child's life and circumstances had been like in the real world. Later in the 1990s, revisions to child-assessment tools would adopt this wider approach and improve those tools' reliability and validity. For a child, no single source of information could ever be the gold standard.

Six weeks after his admission, David was found cutting into a sore on the back of his wrist. His social worker indicated in David's progress notes that he continued to enjoy the "shock value" of talking about suicide. One day later, David attempted to escape from Eufaula. He was locked in "time out" for eight hours as a punishment.

Five days after his attempted escape, David cut his arm with a piece of metal. He was found standing in the bathroom on his ward, his left arm in the sink with the water running, and bleeding profusely. David was taken to the Lakeview Community Hospital emergency room and given ten stitches. Back at Eufaula, his social worker described the wound as "fairly lethal due to vertical, wide cut and possibility of loss of excessive blood." Staff called one of the consulting psychiatrists to inform him that David had pulled the sutures out with his teeth. The psychiatrist did not speak with or visit the boy. Over the phone, he prescribed him 25 mg of Vistaril, a tranquilizer. David returned to the Lakeview ER and was sutured up again. Ward staff put him in restraints that evening. Again, no one called his parents.

A week later, ward staff placed David in seclusion again for "failure to follow rules, bleeding on the walls, and defecating on the floor of the 'time out' room." No therapist or doctor met with the boy. David arrived at Lakeview for a third time. He had stabbed a pencil into his arm. The Lakeview physician had already treated David twice and requested that a psychiatrist evaluate the boy. The hospital psychiatrist gave Eufaula clear instructions, writing: "This child MUST be evaluated for antipsychotic medication."

A second Eufaula psychiatrist examined David the following day. His brief notes in David's chart stated the following: "This young man has been engaging in self-destructive behavior. Case reviewed with therapist and nurse. No current or past evidence of psychosis. MS: alert, oriented. Thought orderly. Affect indifferent. Memory and intellect intact. This difficulty seems behavioral." David's treatment plan was not changed, and again, no one called David's parents.

Chapter Sixteen

Eight months into my new job, I headed to Eufaula. Brenda had recommended I wear jeans and sneakers. "Children will take to you more easily," she told me. She might've been right, but I preferred the reassurance of a business suit in dealing with staff. I hadn't forgotten the trip to Bryce Hospital, where the tour wasn't just defensive but openly hostile.

Before MacLaren released me, I had tried to run away. I hadn't thought it through. There was no plan. It was instinct that made me do it. I was a small, skinny kid waiting for my mom to take me home. I was almost eight years old and had been at MacLaren for nearly a year. Out of the blue, I ran for the fences as fast and hard as I could. Looking out at the miles of scrub farmland surrounding MacLaren, I began climbing and was nearly at the top. One of the orderlies climbed up after me, and as he yanked at my foot, my wrist dragged across the barbed wire. I still have a three-inch razor-thin scar to show for it. He threw me to the ground, but for the life of me, I couldn't recall what happened next. I couldn't remember my punishment.

Working with children, I later learned that the most concerning ones weren't those who cried or threw tantrums. Instead, it was the silent ones—children who had lost faith in adults' ability to protect them. They were the children who had given up. I knew because I was nearly one of them. After only a few months at MacLaren, I had stopped talking.

From the Columbus Airport in Georgia, the fifty-mile drive south to Eufaula took less than an hour. I pulled into the institution's parking lot, forty minutes before my scheduled one o'clock arrival. Tapping the steering wheel with the entrance gate waiting behind me, I stared at the dashboard clock, taking in every minute of extra time. Outside, the scent of the piney woods filled the air.

Stepping into what resembled the interior of a prefab trailer, my eyes adjusted from the sunlight outside. The tiled floor felt weak beneath my feet as I approached an older woman. After several seconds, she broke from her paperwork and gave me a dead smile. "May I help you, young man?"

"Yes." Through the window at her back, sunlight glinted off the razor wire rolling over the fence. "My name is Andrew Bridge."

She eyed me silently.

"I'm here for a tour. I'm with the *Wyatt* lawsuit."

"Take a seat," she answered sharply, pointing to the sofa behind me. "I'll get the clinical director." She shoved open the side door, where the grainy images of a half dozen surveillance cameras flickered over the parking lot outside, low-slung buildings on the property, and what had to be miles of fencing.

I tucked my briefcase at my feet. A collection of framed certificates of operation hung on the wood paneling, along with a print of the town's artificial lake that attracted tourists in the summer.

I recognized the photo from marketing brochures produced to entice parents to send their children to the institution, claiming Eufaula offered a summer camp. The only "camp" for Eufaula's children was a caged compound isolated from everything they knew. And the brochures certainly didn't mention that Eufaula was always full because the more beds that children occupied, the more money the institution received from the state.

Alabama was not a rich state to begin with, and Barbour County, where Eufaula is situated, was perennially among the ten poorest of the state's sixty-seven counties. Seen by locals as a valuable economic opportunity, the institution was packed with administrators, frontline staff, groundskeepers, and more. Eufaula was one of the largest employers for miles around. The facility was allotted $11,000 per month for every child sent there, with over half of that money going to salaries. Across the state, the median household income was under $16,000 a year. Eufaula offered the rarest of commodities in Barbour County: stable work with a good salary.

The side door flew open, and a heavyset man appeared. Dressed in shirtsleeves, his face red from the sun, the facility's apparent clinical director stepped to the middle of the room. He waited for me to stand.

"Good morning, sir. I'm one of the lawyers in the lawsuit. My name is Andrew—"

"I know who you are," he interrupted. "What do you want?"

"I think my boss arranged for... I mean I think the attorney general's office called, said I was coming."

He scoffed. "I asked you what you need."

I felt myself take a step back. "Do you think we could walk around a little? Talk to some of my clients here?"

"They're at lunch."

I remembered the children's schedules from the documents I had reviewed. "It's about quarter past one, and lunch goes to two thirty, right?"

He ran his forefinger across his sweaty brow. "Then you should know after lunch we get 'em back in the gym for physical education, line 'em up in the wards at four for showers—"

"Before the evening shift changes at five p.m.," I interrupted. Holding my expression firm, I scratched at the handle on my briefcase. "I've read the schedules. It's a long lunch."

"You wanna feed them?" he snapped back.

Knowing what he'd gain from a confrontation and his report back to Montgomery, I smiled. "Do you think we could head to the cafeteria, then?"

He turned toward the woman behind her desk. "Looks like I need to take Counselor..." He turned his eyes back at me, running his tongue under his lip.

"Bridge," I interjected.

"I need to take Counselor Bridge to the cafeteria. Apparently, he has a legal need to observe how residents eat."

He unlocked the side door, muttered, "And if you're thinking about a school or ward visit today, ain't happening."

Brenda and Jerry couldn't have been clearer. I was not to interrupt schedules or disturb operations under any circumstances. Facilities needed to remain open to our experts and us. Alabama could shut that down at any point, cutting off contact with our clients at every institution. If I gave them an excuse to complain, my visit could be the one that brought everything to an immediate halt.

"That won't be a problem, sir," I answered with a nod.

Leading the way through a string of corridors, the man walked out an exit into a landscape of near-perfect green and clumps of dull, squat buildings.

Little had changed since officials in Montgomery had acquired the property twenty-three years earlier. Like the military base it had been, everything was meticulously clean on the outside—bushes trimmed, leaves swept. Except for a few hangar-size corrugated warehouses, every building was a two- or three-story copy of the same boxlike structure, all painted beige. I caught up to my escort's side. "I'm sorry. I didn't get your name."

"Because I didn't give it to you." We passed the corner of an administrative building, crossing the lawn.

As the two of us walked out of sight of the reception trailer, there was no sign of the boys and girls housed here. There wasn't a bicycle or a ball. No scrap of forgotten paper or wad of gum like an average middle school. These grounds were empty and quiet. With the director in the lead, I noticed the only construction that may have been built for children, a fenced and drained pool, its faint blue floor empty but for dirt and dead leaves.

He crossed the lawn toward an asphalt courtyard perched on a spot of high ground, walled by two dormitories directly on either side. As I rushed to follow, we passed two wooden posts beside each building, one marked Girls, the other Boys. Girls were lodged two or three to a room in the former officers' quarters. Boys were confined to the smaller rooms in what had been the enlisted men's barracks. We passed through the courtyard, and he broke away to unlock a double metal door leading into another building. Inside the dimly lit corridor, we made our way forward.

"Well, head on in," he snapped. Then as an afterthought, he finally said, "My name is Carlton; that's *Dr.* Carlton."

I entered the cafeteria and walked toward the first circle of tables. The room reeked of teenage perspiration. With Carlton behind me, the clamoring voices halted. What appeared to be twenty or so frontline male staff lined the circumference of the room. The children sat by themselves at the tables, a withdrawn group with white-bread sandwiches, half-eaten apples, and half pints of milk littered around them.

One look at those orderlies and MacLaren barreled back at me. Hundreds of frightened children jammed into the cafeteria for our meals, all of us clamoring down the long tables for our food trays. All of us under the watchful eyes of staff guarding the exits, slouched like bored bullies. The dank, weeping steam of an institutional lunch slopped onto hundreds of plates, and the air thick with the smell of fried bologna and rancid milk.

I moved in closer, and a soft murmur grew. Inviting me to sit, children scooted to the side. Others remained as they were, motionless at their food trays. With the staff glowering from the walls, I squeezed into a table and raised my hand with a small wave. "Hello, my name is Andrew." Children nodded back at me. Others looked away. Across the table, an older boy with a scar running the width of his forehead asked, twisting his green tank top, "What's your name again?"

"I'm Andrew, Andrew Bridge." I reached for my suit jacket pocket, spread out a stack of business cards that I had brought from the office.

"You ain't from here. I can tell by your voice," an older girl yelled out. Her face was covered in freckles.

"Yes, that's right. I'm from Washington, DC. Where are you from?"

She grinned with an overbite. "I'm from Marion. It's on the other side of Montgomery from here. My daddy lives there."

I reached for more business cards, "Does the rest of your family live there with him?"

She rolled her eyes. "Only my daddy. We ain't got nobody else."

Whether the white girl knew it or not, she and her father lived in the state's "black belt," a swath of territory extending across the heartland of the South, named for its dark, fertile soil. It was known formerly for plantations, now for soaring rates of poverty among Black and white citizens alike. Of the children in the room, I counted fewer than twenty Black children. I knew to look. Our expert and I had dug through basic indices of children's ages and races. They were one of the few documents that the state had provided; we were surprised to get them and thought they had been sent by mistake. The pages indicated where children came from when they arrived at Eufaula and where they went when they left.

We arrived consistently at the same disparity in race: children entering Eufaula were overwhelmingly white, and of the few Black children who did come, they were transferred disproportionately to one of the state's juvenile detention facilities.

A younger boy reached for a card. "What are those?"

I slid one closer, knelt to him. "It has my name, the place where I work with the phone number and address. It's where you can reach me if you want. I can also call any one of you. I promise."

Mulling it over, the boy tilted the card under the light.

I would've been surprised to get a call. If a child could access a phone, staff would immediately ask what they were doing. The moment the child answered, "I'm calling Andrew Bridge," the phone would be taken. But the point was I wanted them to remember my name and trust that I was coming back.

The girl from Marion bumped her shoulder against one of the girls next to her. The teenager was a heavyset girl wearing a tight white T-shirt with writing blazed on it—something that looked like it could've been picked up at a roadside convenience store. She gazed up behind a pair of thick-framed glasses with boyishly cut bangs.

Straightening up in her chair, she corrected her shirt with a quick tug. I glanced at the cloth stretched tightly over her torso and read the printed sign across her chest: "OBJECTS behind this T-shirt are LARGER than they appear." I paused. "How old are you?"

"I'm fifteen."

I reached to shake her hand, surprised she wasn't older. "What's your name?"

"Kimberly." She pushed closer into her friend, hesitating to take my hand.

"It's good to meet you, Kimberly." I dropped my arm and looked down at her shirt. "Do you mostly wear clothes you brought from home?"

She pressed her chin against her neck, peered down at her chest, said formally, "The staff got me this for my birthday."

I glanced over my shoulder at Carlton and the men at his side. Under my knotted tie, I tugged at my moist collar.

"Where are you from, Kimberly? Do you live with your parents?"

She smiled at me, cupped her hand to her friend's ear, whispered in giggles. Noticing every card had vanished, I reached for a second stack. "Would you like one?" Kimberly shook her head. I held a card out to her friend. "Would you take it for her? An extra, in case she changes her mind."

A round-faced boy rocking in his chair at a smaller table alone threw out, "Ain't you young to be a lawyer?" He fingered what looked like a sugared gummy worm from his pant pocket, then stuffed it inside his cheek like a wad of chewing tobacco. Landing his chair, he propped his elbows on his cutoff jeans. "Did they hire you? Who says you're coming back?"

Carlton and the others stepped closer.

"No, they didn't hire me. I don't work for them. I don't work for Eufaula. I'm your lawyer, not theirs." Avoiding the faces of the staff encircling us, I followed up, "I'm part of a lawsuit about you. It's about where you came from, how you got here. I'm here to find out what all this is like for you." I paused, then said, "I'm coming back because I want to."

Carlton reached over and dropped his hands on the boy's shoulders. With his eyes locked on me, the man's tone was overbearing. "Joshua, I think you've asked the lawyer here enough. He doesn't have much time to stay."

Joshua twisted under Carlton's grasp. Grinning sheepishly, he fingered the saliva-covered thing out from his mouth. "You want it?" he asked. "I got more in my room."

I looked closer at what was a black-segmented rubber lure with a hooked lime-green tail. "Thank you." I dropped it inside my suit pocket. "I can always use some good bait. Where'd you get it?"

Before Joshua could answer, a high-pitched voice interrupted, "How long are you staying?" I turned in its direction and, from the next table, caught sight of a small boy wedged between two older girls. "I said, are you staying here for a while?" he repeated, as one of the girls rubbed her hand over his buzz-cut blond hair.

I dropped my palms in the middle of the table. "A few days, but I hope to get to know you some."

Grabbing the blond boy like a doll, the girl wrapped her arms around the neck of his mustard-yellow polo shirt. "You two look like brothers," she teased, pulling him tighter. He tugged away from the girl's hold.

"What's your name?" I asked.

"Wayne Alton Tatum," he responded with a clarity that almost seemed rehearsed. "Are you gonna talk with me while you're here?"

"Of course, we can talk."

"My grandma Colleen lives in Andalusia, that ain't near Marion." To a ripple of laughter, he glanced toward the girl behind me. "I'm thirteen."

As I turned to the table beside us, he volunteered loud enough for Carlton and the staff to hear, "You know, I ain't never been locked up before."

I responded with a lie. "Well, that makes two of us."

Children introduced themselves as I passed, occasionally volunteering the name of a child who did not. Taking my hand, they offered the places they came from across the state: Opelika, Monroeville, Birmingham, Alabaster, Selma, Anniston, Opp, Huntsville, Wetumpka, Montgomery, and others. Most of them ignored Carlton and the staff pressed at my back.

Forgetting the time, I sat at a full table near the room's edge. An older girl tapped her elbow against me and grinned, before whispering something I couldn't make out to her friend. "I think that's enough for the day, Counselor," Carlton hissed in my ear, "if you're done recruiting clients." Holding my smile on the children in front of me, I whispered in reply, "They're already my clients, Doctor."

I glanced at my watch. It was nearly half past two, and the room was feeling antsy. Children and the frontline staff were waiting for the gym, followed by showers at four and the shift change at five.

I walked next to Carlton down the dim corridor leading the way outside. "I'd like to see the school, look at the dorms, talk to the kids privately in their rooms."

He said nothing. Crossing the courtyard and lawns, we approached the institution's first building. I turned toward the door I had exited earlier in the afternoon, pacing across the sand road. He pointed to the front gate and razor wire. "You ain't going back through our offices. You can leave like your clients do."

Chapter Seventeen

"Would you like to inspect the room?" the woman at the check-in desk at my motel asked. I leaned toward her and politely declined.

"What about turning on the telephone?" She looked up. "There's an extra charge."

"Yes, thank you. I'll need to call the office soon." I slid my credit card and driver's license to her. Her nails clicking on the computer monitor, she asked what brought me to town. I mentioned visiting Eufaula.

She nodded. "I think about the children there sometimes ... no family. You know they use prison dogs when the kids try to run?"

"Dogs?" I asked, unsure whether to believe her.

"Yeah, they do." She dropped my license and room key into a metal tray. "They get 'em from the men's prison at Ventress. Those are children, not grown male prisoners. I don't give a damn about the jobs that place has."

I signed the paperwork and picked up my bag. The older woman held her eyes on me as I turned for my room. "You take care of yourself, young man. You're a long way from home."

The ring startled me awake the next morning. I looked up at the television, realizing I must've left it on in the middle of the night. The phone rang again.

It was Brenda.

"What on earth did you do?" she asked, laughing.

"I'm sorry?" I rubbed my eyes in the sunlight. "What do you mean, 'what did I do?'"

"Alabama's counsel filed another motion about you. They know how to pump them out. This one they even called about after they sent the fax." She whistled. "Motion for a Protective Order Regarding Andrew Bridge," she recited. "Apparently, you have an interest in adolescent girls."

"What?" I took a deep breath. "I think you know that's a lie."

"Well, staff noticed you talked to a few yesterday."

"In the middle of a crowded lunchroom," I interjected.

"They devoted an entire page to the impropriety of a grown man wanting to meet with teenage girls alone."

"Is that right?" Fumbling to get dressed, I noticed the suit I'd thrown on the floor. "I can't talk to girls alone? Are they aware of the right to speak privately with counsel? Is this the twentieth century?"

"We negotiated a solution, after a forty-five-minute argument. You can speak privately with the girls on the institution's open grounds in full view of others or inside the administrative building's main conference room."

"You mean where I can be checked on?"

"Well, you could think of it that way," she said wryly. "Listen, you're fine. They're a gang of idiots. How was yesterday? We thought about you when you didn't call."

"It went all right, I hope. I think the kids might trust me."

"That's a good start."

"Yeah." I glanced out the window at the rental car. "Thanks, I gotta go."

"One last thing," she interrupted. "We thought it'd be helpful if a legal assistant from local counsel came down. Call it another set of eyes. A witness if necessary. We also thought she could videotape your interviews with children. Her name is Megan. Too late for this time, but next trip, she'll be there."

"Thank you."

Chapter Eighteen

Kimberly's brown hair was cut boyishly short, parted carefully down the middle. She wore an oversize white T-shirt that hung from her neck to the ragged ends of her cutoff jeans.

As I reached for my notes, her first words were, "I want a shower curtain."

"Of course." The interruption caught me off guard. "We can get to that, I promise. Do you remember my name?"

"Andrew… Andrew Bridge." Her voice was slight, high-pitched.

"Do you know what a plaintiff is?" I asked.

"I'm not sure, but it's about courts," she answered.

"That's right, it's the person who brings a lawsuit. You're a plaintiff, right now, in a lawsuit about how you're treated here. I've said it earlier, but I'm a lawyer. I work on a lawsuit called *Wyatt*. I'm one of the lawyers representing every boy and girl here." While I waited for her to show she understood, she gazed at the fluorescent lights on the conference room ceiling. "I won't tell anyone here anything you tell me. Okay?"

"Okay," she whispered, still looking up at the stained ceiling tiles.

"All right, I know your first name, but could you tell me your full name and age?"

She turned to me. "Kimberly Leslie Marks." Then she reminded me what she'd told me in the lunchroom. She was fifteen.

Jotting down her name and age, I asked, "Where were you before Eufaula?"

"I was home."

"And where's home? I don't think we had a chance to talk about that yesterday."

"Autauga County, Prattville." She clasped her hands in front of her.

I smiled. "Do you live with your mom and dad there?"

"Just my mom. The state told my dad to move out. My mom's got boyfriends. I'm not good at names. They come and go." I took another note.

"What does she do for work?"

She shrugged. "She picked for a while."

"Picked?" I asked.

"Wire, aluminum, bricks from ripped-down buildings. I'm not sure what she does now."

"Why did the judge order you here to Eufaula?"

Kimberly shot me a quick look. "I'm voluntary."

"You mean your mother put you here and not the court?"

She nodded.

"Oh, I got it wrong." I glanced down at her torn sneakers, thinking that children placed voluntarily by their parents arrived with street clothes packed from home. Her white T-shirt and plain jeans implied involuntary removal, usually a sheriff and social worker arriving unannounced, hustling the child away without time to pack. Clothes were important. They gave children something that was theirs, a connection to a home before Eufaula.

But I heard the tone in Kimberly's voice, saw the hurt in her eyes. She was old enough to understand that voluntary was a legal status, a technicality that told her she was free to leave. She had that choice, even if there was no place for her to go. That really wasn't the point. Kimberly knew—and wanted me to know—that voluntary meant her mother knew where she was. Her authority hadn't been taken. Her mom could step in and protect her. Kimberly had a mother, in the fullest sense. That's what she needed me to know.

"I'm sorry, that was my mistake," I continued. "How did you get here? I mean, what happened the day you arrived?"

"My mom said we was going to the lake, but took me here instead."

"Why was that?" I followed up.

"For suicide attempts."

I jotted down "suicide attempts."

Kimberly read what I had written.

"I didn't ask if I could take notes." I tapped my fingers against my forehead, worried what to do next. "I'm sorry. I should've done that."

"It's okay, I's just nosy."

I looked down at the notepad, placed my pen to the side. "Kimberly, how many adults have interviewed you, people like me who you've never met before?"

She thought for a moment, then answered blankly. "I ain't sure. Twenty-five, maybe thirty."

I was just another stranger sent to parcel out Kimberly's life. I knew the feeling. By the time I got to fifth grade, I had repeated what had happened to Mom and me so many times that recounting it left me bored and irritated.

I smiled at Kimberly's small eyes and rolled back from her in my chair. "We can stop. We don't have to do this. I won't be upset. I promise. We can talk about anything you want."

"It doesn't matter. You can ask me whatever you like." She tugged at her shorts and held her tone even. "You're fine, Mr. Bridge."

I pulled my questions closer and went on to the next one. "Kimberly, did anyone explain what has to happen before you can leave?"

"I have to not want to hurt myself because when I'm angry or depressed, I want to hurt myself."

"Where are you going after Eufaula?"

"Home."

"You mean to your mom?"

She smiled mutely.

"Is that what the staff told you," I went on. "You were going back home?"

"No, I know I'm going back home." She held her eyes steadily on me.

"Has the staff talked with you at all about that?"

"No."

"What are the staff's plans for you?"

She shook her head. "I dunno." Outside the conference room's double glass doors, an adult voice shouted at one of the children to fall into line. The staff must have been emptying the school for lunch.

"What does your case plan say?"

"I haven't seen that." She looked confused.

"Okay." I continued, "Do you have therapy?"

"Group."

"Any individual therapy?" I interjected. "Someone to talk to about why your mom wanted you here?"

She tapped her glasses up her nose. "Individual therapy lasts a half hour, every week."

"Are you taking any medication?"

"Zoloft, lorazepam, and two other meds."

"Why do you take those medications?"

"The Zoloft is for my attitude and to help my depression, because if I don't take it"—she looked down—"if I don't take it I get mad and take my anger out on other people. Zoloft keeps me going."

I looked to the side. "Do you ever not take your medication?"

"No," she answered defensively.

"Do any kids not take their meds?"

"No," she repeated before correcting herself. Children didn't always swallow their meds but took them back to their rooms. Caplets or solid pills were crushed and sniffed. The others were just swallowed. A girl had given a boy nearly a week's worth of Prozac. They snorted it together.

"Does Dr. Carlton ever find out?" I asked.

"Yes."

"What happens?"

"He gets mad." Kimberly slid her chair from me, gazing to the side. "He sends you to B-Mod." Her words were formal, institutional speak. "Staff do it on their own sometimes."

"I'm sorry, where is B-Mod?" I asked.

"It's the basement of the boys' ward. There's a row of empty rooms with a mattress and a blanket."

"Does Dr. Carlton or staff tell a child how long they'll be in the basement?"

"No," Kimberly answered calmly.

"Once Dr. Carlton orders the child to be put in the basement, does he allow you to go to school or to eat?"

"No, but they'll put a tray in there."

"Is the child alone?"

"Yes, but sometimes a staff person's at the end of the hall. But they don't talk to you, and you can't see them."

I glanced out the door's double windows to the road leading to the children's wards. "Kimberly, have you seen what B-Mod looks like?"

"Yes."

"Has Dr. Carlton or staff put you there?"

She squeezed her knuckles white. "Yes."

"How long have you been there?"

"I think the longest was five days." She blew out her lips. "Hard to keep track."

I reached for the notepad aware my next line of questioning wasn't there. "Kimberly, have you been sad enough to hurt yourself here?"

"Yes. There's broken glass . . . a lot of things to find."

"Do staff find out about that?"

"Sometimes," she answered.

"What do staff do?"

"When it's bad, they take me to the emergency room in town."

I nodded slowly and continued, "And when you come back from the emergency room, where do you go?"

"Staff put me in the basement." She looked straight at me. "Like I said, under the boys' ward."

My eyes warming, I swallowed. "Do you think staff cares about you?"

"No, nobody here cares. Residents, staff make fun of me."

"Who?"

"Besides, like I said I'm not good at men's names." She smiled tightly. "I'd rather not say."

"If you could change anything here," I asked, "is there anything you want?"

"Like I said, I'd like a shower curtain." She looked down at her bare legs. "One for the open stalls on the girls' ward."

"Oh, I'm sorry, Kimberly. A shower curtain," I repeated. "Why is that?"

"I just need to be alone. All I need is privacy from everyone."

"Do you talk to your therapist about wanting a shower curtain?" The question made me feel unsteady, as if it were something too close for a man to ask. I thought of the men coming and going in her home and the names she couldn't remember.

"I don't like to talk about that." She slipped her hands up the opposite arms of her shirt.

Behind the door to the administrative offices, a man burst into laughter, yelling at a coworker, while a phone rang and rang with no one answering. Kimberly ignored the noise.

"Do you tell your therapist why privacy is important to you?"

"I don't think there's a point to that." She cast her eyes at the rows of empty shelves.

I nodded, almost done with the questions. "Before we finish, is there anything you want to ask me? Anything you want to say?"

"No, I don't have anything." She shook her head. "Except I'm better, I'm ready to go home to Mom now." She checked the wall clock. "I need to be getting back. Lunch is started. Staff'll ask why I took so much time here."

Stepping toward the door, her head to the floor, she added, "I'm glad you come."

I turned toward the sunlight. "Kimberly, may I ask one last thing?" She paused, looked into the room. "Why did your mother take you here and not somewhere else, to a doctor for example?"

She took off her glasses, spoke to the empty space. She'd asked why they weren't stopping at the lake. Her mother handed her a brochure and said she didn't know what else to do. The staff here would help her, and besides, they couldn't pay what it would cost anywhere else. While Kimberly looked through the fence, her mom did her best to cheer her up. This place was better than that lousy house in Prattville. There was grass here and an in-ground pool. *They'll make you safe here,* her mom promised. They waited until the gate opened and two male staff took her away. As Kimberly put it, her mom swore to be back once she was better. Kimberly would pull things together. She'd get herself ready.

Chapter Nineteen

We had expected Alabama to fight our discovery requests and they did. Claiming that the lawsuit had been illegitimate from the start, they told the court, in trite TV legalese, that our requests were a "fishing expedition." Our requests had been limited, and they knew that the court would side with us. The waste of time was a strategy.

The state had legions of lawyers—an entire attorney general's office if they wanted it, plus the private firm they had hired. All paid for with the steady flow of taxpayer dollars. We were just a handful of lawyers, and we had to respond to every frivolous motion, every inane objection and dubious court filing that they slapped together.

Even a poor state like Alabama could afford the endless tit-for-tats, the filings and objections that would suck a nonprofit dry.

Our money came from private donations and the occasional grant pried from a foundation that could be convinced to pay the costs of a lawsuit we weren't guaranteed to win. We asked for 140 weeks of children's histories. That would leave out hundreds of children, but it was all we could afford.

Despite the limitations, we were finding enough. There was the disturbing case of Mr. H, a frontline mental health worker responsible for the day-to-day supervision of children on their wards. Shortly after he was hired, Eufaula investigated five separate incidents of physical and sexual misconduct involving him and children in his care. His behavior was widely known at the facility. In his sixth incident, he raped a girl in a bathroom stall. Eufaula's senior administrators interviewed the girl along with a second child who witnessed the assault, concluding both children's interviews corroborated what they had already reported to the staff.

The mother of a former patient called to report that Mr. H was sending her daughter sexually explicit letters, while a fellow staff member revealed that he overheard the man on the telephone arranging to have sex with another girl in the bathroom. Though internal investigators substantiated the first girl's rape, Eufaula's administrators allowed Mr. H to continue working with children for another eight weeks, assigning him to the boy's dormitory. They did nothing to prevent his contact with girls at the institution generally or to halt the risk that a sexual predator posed to any child regardless of sex.

Three days before Mr. H's case was referred to the grand jury, Eufaula's administrators permitted him to resign rather than terminate him. The girl failed to appear at the grand jury hearing, though the facility's records clearly indicated she was a patient at the time. No one bothered to ask why she was not released to testify, and Eufaula did nothing to help her pursue criminal charges. Though it was a mental health facility, Eufaula never offered the child any therapy to address her sexual assault by one of its employees. Once administrators discharged the girl and she left its front gate, Eufaula washed its hands of any responsibility for her assault. Mr. H never faced criminal charges.

Apart from the failure to prosecute Mr. H, his uninterrupted presence sent a clear message to everyone at Eufaula: staff sexual abuse was quietly tolerated. In a deposition that I defended, counsel for the state of Alabama questioned Marci White, our expert, on her view of the incident.

"In your opinion, do you think that the act between the young woman and staff member could have been consensual?" Alabama's counsel inquired.

"I refuse to discuss the possibility that a fifteen-year-old child in a mental institution can consent to sexual intercourse with a male staff member," Marci replied.

Alabama's attorney could have kept going with his questions, insisting that under the rules for deposing a witness, our expert was required to answer what he asked. He dropped the matter, asked for a break, and left the room. With the two of us alone, Marci turned to the stenographer's empty chair and remarked laconically, "I don't lie and I don't do stupid."

The girl who was assaulted was fifteen—Kimberly's age. Kimberly's mother had no way of knowing what was going on inside the facility where she had voluntarily taken her daughter in order to protect her from hurting herself. Yet given the way Eufaula's administrators handled sexual assault, Kimberly was no safer than she had been at home.

Most of the children at Eufaula were, like Kimberly, voluntarily admitted by their parents. Because no court had ordered their placement formally, voluntary children were free to be discharged at their own or their parents' request—on paper, at least. In practice, that voluntary status was a fiction that became apparent when a parent insisted that they wanted their child back. Kimberly and her mother could have tried walking out of Eufaula, but their chances of getting anywhere were slim. Every child filled a bed, and every filled bed meant money for the institution and salaries for its staff. In a town with fewer than fourteen thousand souls, that mattered a lot.

Outside the institution's main gate, an administrator would meet the parent and child with a fresh court order in hand. Not much was required—a vague allegation regarding a child's behavior, like a failure to follow the rules, or merely an opinion from one of the staff. That was enough to get the discharged child put back inside.

The involuntary nature of commitment proceedings to Bryce Hospital was brought up during the earliest days of the lawsuit. Judge Johnson had ruled that when patients were confined to Bryce without due process protections, at the very least they had to be given adequate treatment. But his ruling had no impact on how patients were sent there in the first place. Commitment hearings were allowed to carry on as they were, and it would take another three years for Johnson to rule that under the United

States Constitution, an accusation of mental illness wasn't enough. An individual had to be psychologically determined to be mentally ill, and there had to be a *real and present threat of substantial harm to himself or others.* As for their defense, they had the right to counsel, and if they were too poor to pay for a lawyer, they had the right to be appointed one. They could call and cross-examine witnesses. They finally were given rights close to what criminal defendants got.

One of the girls told me how her "voluntary status" at Eufaula worked. Her name was Ashley. She was one of the few children from Dothan, not far from the City of Eufaula itself. Her grandmother worked as a file clerk for the Alabama Power Company. Ashley was seventeen years old when I first met her.

On my next trip to the facility, I showed up on a Saturday morning in late January. I had given Alabama two weeks' notice before I flew down from Washington. Jerry had recommended the visit, if only for the day. Like most institutions, Eufaula slimmed down to a skeleton staff from Friday evening to Monday morning. No activities were planned at the available but shuttered on-site school. The result was a volatile mix of too few adults left to supervise too many children, all penned up and desperately bored. Weekends were when Eufaula ran itself. Weekends were also when incidents got out of hand and children got hurt.

Breakfast was over when I arrived. Despite my warning, no administrator had been willing to sacrifice the day off to mind me. Even Carlton wasn't available to do it. There was only the frontline staff, and one of them escorted me into the gym. The scent of turpentine rose from the gleaming floor. From the look of it, nearly all of Eufaula's 120 children had been crowded inside. About half of the children were scattered around the bleachers; the others had gathered into groups of varying numbers alongside the walls. The employees had retreated into their cliques around the entrance and just outside. No one was shooting baskets or kicking around a ball or, for that matter, doing anything that the place was built for. The gym was a holding tank filled with teenagers and echoing with loud, uneasy noise.

Seated as high as she could, one of the older girls was staring straight ahead. If she knew anyone, she wasn't showing it. I made my way up, tapping kids on the back and saying hellos. The air-conditioning overhead was blowing full blast, and her hand was cold when I reached over. "I'm Andrew Bridge, are you okay? Did you want to be up here on your own?" Her auburn hair was pulled back, and her button-down shirt was freshly ironed.

"That's all right, you can stay, sir." She was fighting back tears. Then she introduced herself as Ashley.

We sat side by side under the canister lighting. Kids were breaking into shoving matches, settling most of them among themselves. Staff was coming and going for what looked like cigarette breaks.

"You know, I don't think I've seen you before," I said. "How long have you been here?"

"I've only been here for three weeks," she said. "My grandmother Helen said it would be good for me."

"What about your parents?"

A screaming match erupted between two girls below us. A couple of boys pulled the two apart—the staff hadn't moved.

"I don't like talking about my mother." Ashley's tone was stiff. "She's up in Selma on her own." I nodded, letting the matter go. The girl's eyes softened. "It's okay. I love my grandmother more than anything." Whatever had happened, Helen took in Ashley and her little sister, enrolled them in school, and adopted the two children.

"Can we talk about why you're here?" I asked.

Ashley had stolen eighty dollars from her grandmother's purse. "It wasn't right to do," she confessed, "not to my grandmother." She had paid her back by doing chores around the house. But there were other things before that. Sneaking out of the house, a cigarette here and there, skipping school, and at one point, she took Helen's car without permission. "All of it built up." Her voice cracked. "Then the eighty dollars pushed it over the edge. That's how I got here."

One week later, Helen drove Ashley to the institution. She told her granddaughter that she was free to walk out of Eufaula anytime. Or Helen could just come get her. Ashley watched while her grandmother reviewed the admission form and checked the box beside "Voluntary Patient."

After David Dolihite left the facility, Montgomery decided to add an on-site patient advocate to Eufaula's employee roster. They chose Randy Hanklin for the position. Blond, smiling, and athletic, Hanklin was the only Eufaula employee who made a point of introducing himself to me. He was also aware that children were, as professionals termed it, "cutting on themselves," using shards of glass that littered the campus, and that children openly traded their medications. He knew that staff members restrained children, throwing them face-first onto the pavement. He saw their bruises and black eyes. Hanklin knew children were kept in the basement of the boy's dormitory for days. He was aware of it all and did nothing.

After Helen left, Hanklin had reviewed Ashley's rights with her, handing her a pamphlet full of them. She talked about her grandmother, and Hanklin promised they could use the ward's pay phone as often as they liked. That had to have reassured Ashley and left her feeling less alone. When Ashley asked about being a voluntary patient, Hanklin promised she could sign herself out when she wanted. He might have made a great soccer coach, but as a patient advocate, Hanklin was a flunky and a liar.

Helen called Ashley every day, often several times. Staff complained that she was calling Ashley too much. Helen came for the weekly visits that she was allowed. She brought her granddaughter fresh clothes, magazines, sketch pads, and pencils, even a diary. Helen was not going to let go.

On the Wednesday before I arrived, Helen called Eufaula. She told whoever answered that she was taking Ashley home. Helen was transferred to Ashley's therapist at the facility. She repeated her request: "I want my granddaughter home." The therapist curtly responded, "How do you know that Ashley isn't going to be like she was before she got here?"

The therapist informed Helen that he had read the form she had filled out when Ashley was admitted. There were also notes from one of the administrators who briefly interviewed Helen that same day. From there, the therapist ticked off Ashley's offenses. "It says that she stole your car. She's a school truant and apparently a thief. Eighty dollars from your purse?"

Helen rose to her granddaughter's defense. "Those are private matters, family ones between her and me."

But they weren't, not anymore. "Those are public offenses," the man remarked, "offenses that are reportable to the police or child welfare." All of them had happened on Helen's watch. Then the therapist took it up a notch: "There's another child, a younger girl, in your home."

He hadn't threatened Helen openly. He didn't need to. He had his tone and the power of the state behind it. Helen made several final arguments to take Ashley home, and to each of them, the man calmly replied, "You have no reassurance of that." Ashley was staying where she was.

When Ashley learned of the conversation from her grandmother, she went to the same therapist. He may not have threatened Helen directly, but as Ashley reported, he did with her. Ashley told the man that she was leaving, packing what she had and heading home. "Go ahead, sign yourself out," her therapist told her. She felt a surge of confidence. The man cleared it up for her. "Try signing out, and you'll be sent to Chalkville." At the mention of Chalkville, Ashley gave up.

Chalkville was a correctional facility for girls operated by Alabama's Department of Youth Services. Occupying more than 570 acres outside Birmingham, the facility could house 130 teenage girls at any time. Male guards ran the compound. They watched girls take showers and conducted strip searches. Girls were raped, beaten, and forced to have abortions after being impregnated by guards. Nearly one hundred girls who had been incarcerated at the facility from 1993 to 2001—the same period during which Ashley's therapist had threatened to send her there—came forward in 2001. The lawsuit made national news. The girls and their mothers sued Alabama for $171 million. After years of battling against the girls and their mothers, the state of Alabama winnowed down the number of victim plaintiffs by more than half and settled the lawsuit for $12.5 million in

March 2007. Alabama's attorney general Troy King told the press that the agreement was "good news for the state."

On the morning of January 23, 2012, a tornado ripped through the area, leveling all but four of Chalkville's fifteen buildings. Eighteen girls were still incarcerated there, but none were hurt. Only then did Alabama shut Chalkville down. Ashley was never sent to Chalkville. She was discharged from the facility close to her eighteenth birthday, Eufaula's age limit. Ashley made it home, but only because by law they couldn't keep her any longer.

Chapter Twenty

Dr. Carlton was waiting at the front gate when I pulled up. My last visit had been at the start of the year; now it was the spring.

"It's barely May and you're already back. What do you want this time?" he asked.

"It's good to see you. Hope you enjoyed your holiday," I answered and then got to the point. "Where would the kids be right now?"

"They'd be in school," he answered.

"Do you think we could go see?"

"Certainly. No suit today? But you got your fancy briefcase." He pointed to my side.

We walked past the boys' and girls' dormitories and entered what resembled a small public school.

"I'd like to go into one of the classrooms," I said.

"Which one?"

Classrooms stretched down the hallway, with posters dotting the walls. I told Carlton to choose. He turned to the closest one, the room falling silent as we entered. Children's heads turned toward us, their wet hair combed, varying in age. A young male teacher stood at the front of the class. I quickly counted roughly fifteen boys and girls crowded around tables and scattered at desks.

Carlton gave the teacher a nod, then apologized to "Mr. Werner" for our disturbance, introducing me and pointedly adding where I'd gone to law school.

Eufaula was Jim Werner's first position. He had gone to Troy University, an hour south of Montgomery. "It's no Harvard," he said, grinning. Troy was known for its education program and had been established to train teachers for Alabama's schools more than a century earlier.

"Harvard's overrated," I quipped. The class was descending into a rumble.

"I picked this place because I like the kids," he threw out. "Though they could use a little more schooltime." Carlton ignored the comment. He'd heard it already.

The young teacher hushed the group with one clap. He cast a look over the room and asked if anyone could tell him where Harvard was. No answer. He stepped to a multicolored map of the United States tacked above the chalkboard a few feet away. He ran his palm over New England. "Is Harvard there?" The room remained quiet. "Can anyone give me a guess?" Hands shot in the air, and Werner bent to a girl at the side of the room. She gazed blankly ahead, ignoring him as he touched her shoulder. A younger boy shouted out, "New York City!" then smiled at me.

Werner propped his hands on his hips. "Mr. Bridge, can you tell us?" He retook the head of the class and playfully waved me forward. I answered Massachusetts. "I think if we ask, he'll show us where it is." Navigating to the front, I touched the map's Atlantic corner. "Thank you," he said.

The lesson plan continued. "Let's get back to our times tables. Leslie, tell us seven times three?" The thin girl hesitated before answering correctly. Werner followed up: "Next one, eight times four?" He clapped again for quiet, waited before offering the answer himself. As I watched, he scrambled from child to child with encouraging nods.

Not far from me, I spotted a teenager with a straggly beard. Asking for the boy's permission, I lifted a tattered textbook from his desk. He smiled confidently while I flipped through an outdated book more appropriate for a third- or fourth-grader than the young man beside me. I spread open a page and pointed to a paragraph.

"What's your name? I'm Andrew."

"I'm Travis Moore," he answered softly.

"Could you do me a favor, Travis? Would you read this one for me?" I asked. And it was a favor, asking him to read aloud in the quiet classroom with Carlton and the teacher looking on.

The teenager bent close, stumbling through syllables and into broken words. When I motioned over the page for him to stop, Travis insisted on finishing. I smiled at him. "Thank you, good job." He grinned back at me.

Eufaula's schedules and prior expert reviews showed that Travis and the rest of the children received three hours and forty-five minutes of academic teaching per day, close to half of what they would receive in public schools. Werner wouldn't have known it, but the request for more schooltime had already been raised with Montgomery. The truth was hidden behind Carlton's silence.

Impoverished children, like Travis, arrived with appalling reading levels. Teachers, advisory groups, and prior experts had argued for years that children needed more time for academics and remedial classes. Eufaula's administrators answered that their institution and children were exempt from those educational obligations. Hours would not be extended. The result was clear as day. Eufaula's children grew from early adolescence to adulthood given nothing near the opportunity their peers in the community received.

Seeing that I was about to go, Travis knocked his knee against me suddenly. "I want to go to Harvard. You said I was good as you," he announced as the class looked at us. Werner and Carlton turned. I looked into the boy's eyes and gave him the only truth I could think of: "Yes, you are every bit as good as I am."

Our legal assistant was supposed to be here this time, as Brenda had promised on my first visit. I scanned the parking lot with Carlton behind me. There was no sign of Megan. Wherever she was, no Megan meant no video camera for the children's interviews. I wanted her there as backup, someone to argue my side if Carlton tried pulling something. We needed the videotapes to show our expert what children reported and how they handled themselves. That would be just as important when choosing which children would testify at trial. A child had to appear steady and articulate, to hold up under pressure. That was a lot to ask of a kid.

"Looks like you been left," Carlton snickered.

"She'll be here."

Back inside, he pointed to some picnic tables in the courtyard and left me to wait. I eyed the sloping hill and the scramble of benches against the fence. I bent to the basement windows of the boys' ward, whose view barely rose to my ankles. I rubbed my hand against the mud-splattered glass. No luck—I couldn't make out a thing. An outside stairwell was lit at the farthest end.

Irritated that I'd lost more than thirty minutes holding out for Megan, I turned to see Carlton emerge from the stairwell with a lanky boy.

"If you don't mind, Dr. Carlton, I'd like to talk with that young man." Carlton stepped forward with him. "I'd like to talk to him alone."

Carlton threw his hands in the air. "By all means, Counselor. You do what you need to do." He glanced at the teenager behind him. "Well, git on."

The boy tugged up his baggy jeans but stuck to where he was. "May I talk to you? We can sit over here." I motioned to the bench.

The boy dipped his head.

"Whatever he's told you doesn't matter," I said. "You can talk, and he can't do a thing about it. It won't take long. Then you can keep going with whatever you're doing."

He shook my hand loosely across the picnic table while Carlton paced in the sun. Then he took a seat and pushed his wiry red hair from his face, revealing reluctant eyes and sideburns struggling down his cheeks.

"Are you nervous with him there? I can ask him to move." He shrugged. I pushed aside my briefcase. "Were you in school today? Did I see you with the others?" He answered no.

A girl's scream shot out from the school. "That was a loud one," I joked. "Where are you and Dr. Carlton headed?"

He cupped his hands before his face; his fingernails were ripped raw. The undersides of his forearms were laced with scars.

"Looks like we've got the same bad habit." I flattened my palm, showing my nails bitten to the quick, then I ran my finger down his wrist. "How'd you get those?"

"Glass." He flipped over his arm. "Glass is money here. I use it when I'm alone."

"Where do you find glass?"

"Busted light bulbs, mostly. We trade it."

I paused at his answer. "You know, I'm a lawyer. I can't tell anyone what you tell me." I flipped my notes to cover the names that I'd written down. "Not even who you are."

He smirked and exposed a brown tooth. "All right, I'm Russell, Russell James Cole, and I'm fourteen. I could use me a lawyer."

"How long have you been here?"

"Three months, one week, four days." He watched me write it down. "I'm from Ensley."

"I'm sorry, don't know it."

Ensley was outside Birmingham. "Nothing but an itty-bitty downtown and old steel mills," he clarified.

"Why did you come from home to Eufaula?"

"I didn't come from home. I came from Mount Meigs. You know that one?"

"Yes," I replied quietly. I knew about Meigs, all right. Russell nodded toward Carlton and said grimly, "He's sending me back there."

Lying to the east of Montgomery, the Mount Meigs juvenile correctional facility was run by the Alabama Department of Youth Services. It was a discharge point for children from Eufaula, all with the notation "unsuccessful." As a juvenile justice detention center, Meigs was not a part of the lawsuit, though attorneys in the office were familiar with it. Alabama's "State Federation of Colored Women's Clubs" had established the facility as Mount Meigs Colored Institute in 1888. White children who ran into trouble were dispatched to reform schools exclusively for children; Black children who did the same were incarcerated in adult prisons. The institution was intended to put an end to that. Financial support didn't come easy; with expenses rising and few other options, the state took over the facility in 1911 and promptly renamed it the Alabama Reform School for Negro Juvenile Law Breakers. Meigs was renamed in 1947 as the Alabama Industrial School for Negro Children and again in 1970, after desegregation, as the Alabama Industrial School.

In 1969, one year before the United States Attorney and Department of Justice challenged conditions at Bryce Hospital, both had filed suit over children's conditions inside Meigs. Attorney and expert tours discovered incarcerated children beaten with brooms, mop handles, fan belts, and fists. They worked the fields for the sole purpose of producing income for the institution. Inadequately fed and clothed, the children were frequently raped. One Alabama juvenile probation officer described Meigs as a "slave camp for children" run by "illiterate overseers." The Meigs lawsuit was settled and conditions improved—slightly.

Even now, in the office, the lawyers talked about Meigs's lingering savagery. The dormitories were packed with children. Alabama failed to hire a sufficient number of security guards and frontline staff, and those who were hired were barely trained. Conditions were ripe for violence and well beyond the control of the adults who worked there. Children were left to govern themselves. Meigs was the real-life version of *Lord of the Flies*.

Staff violence against children at Meigs continued for years. In August 1999, a Black seventeen-year-old boy diagnosed as psychotic was transferred to the compound. He had a meltdown two months later. The boy stripped off his clothes in his cell, screaming, "The blood of Jesus is on me" and "Jesus, come get me." He clogged his toilet and flooded the jail deck before attempting to hang himself, but the string broke. Then Meigs officers entered the cell, and children reported hearing the boy being punched or slapped. Next came the sound of choking.

While children watched, officers carried the limp and handcuffed boy past them. One of the men kept repeating, "Damn... damn... damn." Though there was a shorter route to the infirmary, the officers chose the longer one. The trip took fourteen minutes, and the boy was no longer breathing by the time they arrived. Attempts at resuscitating the boy were unsuccessful. All life-support efforts were discontinued at the local hospital. Following the state's failed attempt to dismiss the case against the Meigs officers under the doctrine of qualified immunity, the lawsuit was settled for undisclosed damages.

I kept my voice as calm as I could. "Russell, what do you think of Meigs? Why does Dr. Carlton want to send you back?"

He had gotten into an argument with staff. They had responded aggressively, and there was a faded bruise around his neck. When I asked him to pull down his collar, Russell's tone was apologetic. In their defense, he said it wasn't his first argument. He apologized to the men who hurt him. Above all else, he didn't want to go back to Meigs. He pointed to the line of basement windows. "I said that I'd even go back down to B-Mod."

Russell was nine years old when the state arrived at his mother's house and took him into custody. Since then, the boy had gone from his first foster home in Birmingham to a state-run "High-Intensity Training" boot camp in Prattville. The program focused on military-style discipline. It didn't work. From the Prattville boot camp, Alabama sent Russell to Charter Woods, a psychiatric facility. From there, he was moved to Mountain View, a second psychiatric hospital. Mountain View discharged him to Hill Crest's mental health unit. The mental health professionals on Hill Crest's staff sent him first to a four-month stint at Mount Meigs. Meigs ordered him to Eufaula, and now Eufaula was sending him back. In the five years that the state had been responsible for his care, Russell had traveled through all of Alabama's children's systems: foster care, juvenile justice, and mental health. He had been sent to seven placements and was headed to his eighth.

Carlton was getting impatient. He stepped to the pavement's edge and yelled, "You two boys about done?" I ignored him and kept my eyes on Russell.

"Do you know what the clinical goals on your chart say?"

Russell knew them by heart, and while I watched, he mechanically recited them for me. He needed to resolve his anger issues. He had to correct his oppositional defiance disorder, his major depression, and his self-harmful behaviors. And apparently, Russell was expected to make those changes on his own because Eufaula had no real treatment plan for him—or for any other child there. For Russell, it wasn't about getting better. It was about avoiding punishment.

"I just need to make them happy." His eyes drifted.

I was getting ready to wrap it up when Russell mentioned his mom.

"When they came to my house in Ensley to take me, they told my mom to get in her bedroom. I think they was afraid that she was gonna fight 'em. That she wasn't gonna just let them take me. She didn't put up a fight." He shook his head. "How's she supposed to do that? But you know something weird?"

I waited.

"We walked out the front door, the sheriff, social worker, and me, and I seen all their cars parked out front. My first thought walking across the yard was the neighbors looking out from their windows. After I was gone, what was they gonna whisper when Mom walked outside? What was she gonna say?"

We looked at the mowed grass and tended trees. "Where do you want to go?" I asked.

"I wanna go home," he muttered. "See my friends in Ensley. Tell Mom we'll figure it out this time." He shifted to the end of the table and reached into his back pocket.

Peering at a creased photograph, he lifted it closer. "I was there when my mom's boyfriend took this of her." I gazed at the young woman smoking on a couch, her bare legs folded with her feet on the coffee table's edge.

"Do you ever see her?"

"It was a long time ago." He shrugged. "We talk on the phone when she can."

"You should keep that. Even if she disappointed you."

He slid the photograph back into his pocket.

"Advice from a lawyer from Washington," I added with a warm smile.

I remembered a photo of my mother: the two of us on my bed at my foster parents' house. Her suede coat pressed against my face as she pulled me into her. She'd spiked her black hair. The late afternoon sun was at our backs, and the smell of dinner was drifting through the house. She'd have to leave before we sat down at the kitchen table. It was the only picture I ever had of her. Years later I lost the photo in one of my moves.

A whistle pierced the air, and as I turned, Carlton dropped his fingers from his mouth. Before I could yell back, Russell shook his head and headed toward him. The boy twisted under the weight of Carlton's arm. "We've got things to get done here. Don't we, Russell? Get you up to Meigs."

The boy gave into Carlton's grip and the two began walking away. Suddenly, Russell turned back. "You oughta take a look around Vocational Rehab and Building 112." Carlton pulled the boy tighter, nearly muzzling him. Russell pointed toward the main road and a corrugated warehouse in the distance. Then he yelled again, "Be sure to talk to Wayne Tatum, because everybody likes little Wayne from Andalusia."

The two paced toward the Eufaula's main gate, where the sheriff's car would drive him seventy-five miles north, halfway to Ensley but no closer to his mother or the people he knew. It was hard to tell if Russell understood the legal divide that he was crossing. Carlton certainly understood. The lawsuit had never covered Alabama's prisons or its juvenile justice facilities. Mental health and juvenile justice were entirely separate. With an early morning call to Montgomery and a painless request to transfer Russell from one state system to the next, Carlton had slung the boy outside the reach of the lawsuit and outside of mine. Carlton could have refused to let me talk to Russell. After all, I was interfering with the state's transportation of a patient. But he had picked his battle wisely because he'd already won. The next morning Russell would wake up in a locked unit at Meigs.

Two months after Russell left Eufaula for Mount Meigs, a riot broke out at the facility. A gang of residents beat another boy with bricks, sticks, fists, and whatever else they could find. It wasn't Russell, but it could just as easily have been him—and that's where Eufaula sent him. I wouldn't see Russell for another twelve years.

After Eufaula and Mount Meigs, Russell never made it back to Ensley. Alabama continued to cycle him through juvenile justice facilities and occasional foster homes. He left state care at eighteen, and when I met him again, he was twenty-six years old. I had become friends with James Tucker, our local lead counsel, after the litigation, and Russell had reached out to him. During a visit to Alabama, I asked James if he would take me to see him. Russell was incarcerated at the Ventress Correctional Facility. Built to house medium- to low-security inmates, Ventress was also the prison that provided the dogs to hunt down children who ran from Eufaula. Russell had been arrested on a minor drug charge, and it was the only time he had gotten into trouble as an adult.

I had flown in from New York City and waited in one of Ventress's conference rooms with James. Russell looked confused at the sight of two strange men in business suits as the guard opened the door. He stepped closer, dressed in the thick cotton fatigues of an Alabama convict with his last name and serial number stenciled across his chest. Men dressed in suits and asking for a prisoner usually meant trouble, the worst of which were new charges about to be filed against the inmate. Russell had good reason to be nervous.

I extended my hand and saw that Russell was unshackled for our meeting. I introduced myself and said that we had met at Eufaula. "Mr. Tucker and I both knew you during the Eufaula lawsuit."

James interjected that if he understood correctly, Russell was on the verge of getting out in July. That put him more at ease. "In June," he corrected James. Then he smiled with the nervousness I remembered when he was a boy.

"We appreciate your willingness to spend some time with us," James continued before adding where I had come from.

"I love New York," Russell piped up. The answer surprised me. "Big city. I traveled through there a couple times goin' back and forth between Pennsylvania and Maine... doin' Walmart stuff."

"You were working at Walmart?" I asked.

Russell shook his head. He wasn't working at Walmart. He was building them. "Takes about two months to put one up," he said. He wasn't sure they'd take him back once he was out. "I don't get in any trouble here. I behave myself and talk with only a few people."

Russell had gotten married when he was twenty. He and his wife had gotten into drugs—painkillers. The opioid epidemic was beginning to tear through the country, and Russell and his wife had been swept up in it.

"I cleaned myself up, been clean for little over a year. But my wife didn't want to leave her drugs alone. One day I held up some pills in one hand and the wedding ring in the other. And I let her pick." He shook his head. "She tried to grab both of them."

They had separated, but Russell couldn't bear to leave her alone. He liked to swing by, hang out, and watch some TV. As he put it, the police knocked on the front door one afternoon. They searched the place and found the pills and a vial of crack. Despite all that had happened to him at the hands of the state of Alabama, his childhood spent in prison-like facilities that offered no treatment or hope, Russell took the rap for his wife. He swore the drugs were his and went to prison for it.

"With Eufaula and all those other places I was put in," Russell said, "I guess I hated life. I felt like nobody wanted me." He threw out the names of a couple of lawyers and social workers who had checked on him and done things for him. But that was it.

"Was there anything that would've helped?" I asked. "Something that might've made a difference?"

"I could say if I had a family like everybody else. You don't need a family to make it. There was people here and there. They just wasn't family-family." He looked past James and me. "It doesn't matter though how much a bad life you have. It's what you make it." Russell clung to that hope even at Ventress.

We thanked the young man for his time. Russell replied, "I appreciate that you came. Not many do." Then one of the Ventress guards arrived and shackled Russell and walked him back to his cell.

Chapter Twenty-One

The school's doors slammed open and shut. Ward staff were herding dozens of children into jagged lines. A few smiled and waved while the stragglers were shoved into place. At the edge of the courtyard where the hill crested, boys and girls fanned out toward the fifteen-foot fence rolled with razor wire. Staff stuck to the heights while the children below tightened into clusters or wandered off alone. The kids called it "going down the hill."

Reminding me that he had better things to do than watch me, Carlton returned to his office. "Do whatever you want" were his words. I took him up on it.

"I'd like to take a look," I remarked to the ward staff. Already on break, a few of them shrugged as I headed toward the slope. What were apparent leftovers from the radar base that Eufaula had been, there was a basketball and tennis court. The broken asphalt was covered in tendrils of crabgrass. It didn't matter if any of the kids knew how to play, because there wasn't a ball or racket around. I recognized most of the residents—they knew me by now. There was the laughter of teasing voices.

"Come here, Mr. Bridge," an older boy called over as he waved. A debate was at full throttle. One nodded at me to sit, and the grass pressed against my palms. "He thinks Predator should've won," he scoffed. "It don't matter what it's got. Against Schwarzenegger, it ain't got a fuckin' chance—I mean any chance. It's a movie. He's gotta win."

All eyes were on me. They waited. Too young to be their father, too old for a brother, I shook my head. "I'm not sure. It's a tough one." Groans flew back at me. "All right, I'll go with Arnold." A couple of smug grins told me I'd done okay; then while I watched, the discussion continued. Bored with Schwarzenegger, the boys jumped to the inevitable: gossiping about girls a few feet away.

While I marched back up toward the staff, a child's voice hit the warm air. "You remember me?" A boy was hunched in the tree overhead. Squinting against the sun, I shouted toward him, "I do."

"Bet you can't remember my name." He threw down a fistful of leaves.

I rounded the trunk closer to him. "Your name is Joshua. Dr. Carlton introduced us in the lunchroom. You didn't tell me how old you are."

He answered that he had just turned twelve, and I asked if he'd like to talk. He twisted on the branch toward the chattering teenagers behind us, then pointed at the staff ahead and told me to ask them.

"Would you like me to wait?" I pressed my hand against the bark. "Maybe I could get you down? You know, you might slip."

"I ain't slipping, and I ain't coming down 'til you ask."

"All right, Joshua. Fair enough."

I trudged up to the staff who stood chatting on the lawn. "Excuse me, there's a boy in a tree down there." I pointed toward the fence. "Would you mind helping him and taking him to the main conference room?" No one responded. "His name is Joshua," I pressed. "He's agreed to speak with me."

One of the orderlies got up from the grass, stepped into me. The musk of cigarettes wafted from him. "We know who the hell that boy is."

I backed away and glanced at my watch. The day was getting late. "I need to talk to him. Could you get him to the conference room in fifteen minutes?" My heart was racing, but I calmly added, "The boy is my client, and I'm asking to speak with him." The man stalked off toward his colleagues.

If she hadn't been fumbling with a camera's tripod in the conference room corner, I wouldn't have had any idea who the twenty-something woman was. She looked up. "I'm guessing you're Andrew," she said. "I'm Megan, the legal assistant from Montgomery. They said y'all wanted to record some kids." I stepped over to give her a hand, but she shook her head. "I got it, Andrew. No wonder they put you in here. This room smells bad enough to gag a maggot. Well, where's the first kid?"

Joshua stepped inside nearly a half hour later. Beside me, the boy swirled in his chair, his shoes barely swiping the floor. He was wearing jeans, black sneakers, and a cartoon shirt, this one with

Looney Tunes splashed across it. After a round of several more spins, he halted, landing his large hazel eyes on Megan and then me.

Joshua was the youngest child at Eufaula.

I closed my eyes. The confrontation with the orderly had been minor, and besides, the boy was now grinning next to me, excited to get talking. But after I had finished and flown home, Joshua would be left to that man.

Megan marched through the interior door that led to the administrative offices, not bothering to knock, and returned with two Dixie cups filled to the rim. She set them down in front of Joshua and me. Returning to the camera, she pressed "record" and the pinprick bulb went red.

Joshua straightened his eyeglasses, making it clear that he was ready. "Was I on the list of kids you was supposed to talk to?" he asked.

"Why would you think that you were on a list?"

"Dunno." He looked at the camera. "Whenever people come, they always want to ask me questions."

"Where are you from, Joshua?" I pushed the conversation forward.

"Bay Minette. You know it?"

"I'm thinking east of—"

"East of Mobile...You got that one right, Mr. Bridge." He grinned. Joshua wanted me to like him.

I reached for my notes. "Joshua, have you taken medications here or before?"

"Thorazine, Tegretol, Ritalin, Haldol, and something to keep me from farting so much. That pill's for farting 'cause it's thicker and tastes good." He giggled.

From stints living with an aunt and uncle to foster families to psychiatric hospitals and Eufaula, Joshua had gone through diets of medications, recalling they changed but not remembering all their names.

"Why did they change?"

He guessed aloud, "They must not have been working?"

"Are the new ones working?" I asked softly.

"I think so. They tell me that."

"Do you always take your meds?"

"No, I have me a whole box of meds from stuffing it in my cheeks. I trade them." He bounced in his chair. "I got myself a Matchbox racer that someone's parent brought." He rolled his chair closer. "I can do something. I got me a trick. You wanna see?"

"Sure, show me," I said.

Holding out his palm between us, he bent both thumbs flat against his wrist. The boy's eyes went somber. "Told you I could do something."

"I bet you can do a lot." I waited before shifting topics. "Does anyone bring you clothes? Are you allowed visitors?"

"I guess, but nobody ever comes excepting people like you." He looked at Megan and then me.

"What do you talk about?" I asked.

"I like fighting. I love fights." He drummed his fingers against the table's edge.

"How many fights do you have in a week?"

"I dunno, eight or ten? I wanna fight." He pushed his glasses up with the ball of his hand and swerved in my direction.

"What else do you like?" I rubbed my thumb against the waxed paper cup.

"Nintendo and climbing trees."

I shifted his chair back into place. "If you're fighting, what does the staff do?"

"I don't like being alone with them. You gotta stay where people see you."

It wasn't quite an answer. "What does restraint look like? And has the staff ever hurt you, Joshua?"

According to Joshua, restraint was whatever staff said it was. And it could be just as troubling as that. Restraint was a broad category, one that included anything from locking a child in a seclusion room to medicating him into submission, or shackling or throwing the child to the floor. It was controversial and always had been. Once physical restraint was allowed, there was no going back. Experts would go on to question whether facility staff ought to be allowed to use it at all.

The thing about physical restraint was that it required constant monitoring and reporting—and well-trained professionals to carry it out. But nurses were expensive and hard to find. A great many of the people employed on facility wards had no experience working with children. This was work that people took for the paycheck. Often the only qualification was a willingness to do it.

These frontline workers needed to have the capacity to assess the difference between a risk and an actual threat. A child telling a staff member to "go fuck yourself" presented a risk, but it was a small one. A child wielding a chair or a piece of glass was a threat. Staff needed to understand the difference. They had to remember that they were the ones in charge; it was up to them to work their way to the safest outcome for everyone: de-escalation. But that meant training, and training cost money.

The leading policy journal on children in state care had published strict licensing requirements for the use of physical restraint in residential facilities. Our expert, Marci White, had gone through the existing parameters of it. Never grab a child's arms, legs, or head. Never pin a child's face down, prone on the ground, or apply pressure on his chest, heart, or lungs.

Actual techniques varied and demanded strict time limits, but some things were clear: two or more staff members had to be involved in any action, and the child was to be monitored constantly. Was the child in any physical danger? What was the child's emotional state? Physical restraint had one constant goal: ending it as quickly as the child's behavior allowed. If someone was hurt, then the entire point of the restraint had failed.

Even after that, Pandora's box was still open.

Taken down once, a child was more likely to be restrained in the future, with the result that a small group of children accounted for an overwhelming number of incidents. Cross that line once and it was easier to cross a second time. And a third. Younger children were restrained more often than older, boys more than girls. Children with a developmental disability were more vulnerable, as were those who were depressed, anxious, or suicidal. Children with histories of trauma and current or former foster children were also at risk. And any number of those characteristics applied to Joshua.

The reality was that staff could and did fabricate threats, then descended on a child for no good reason. What's more, an attitude of "tough love" developed among staff, as if restraining a child, even excessively, showed how much they cared. New staff members tended to follow the highly physical tactics older staff used to control children. That also meant less aggressive, strictly verbal means of exerting control fell by the wayside. Left unreported and without review, physical force became normalized at the facility. Everyone was gradually indoctrinated into "a tradition of toughness." The stage was set for a facility where violence was not only allowed but expected.

Joshua propped his foot on his chair and began tightening one of his shoelaces.

"When staff is upset with you, do you go to your room and wait?"

"The rooms ain't got locks." The twelve-year-old went for the other sneaker. "When they come at you screaming down the hall, you gotta barricade and stop them from getting at you."

Joshua described how he started with the mattress over the ward room door. As fast as he could, he hoisted the bed frame against it and hauled the desk across the floor. He was small, and it had to have taken all that he had. Then he went for everything, his clothes and the hangers, the empty suitcase helped. Once he finished, he balled himself up inside the closet.

"The closet's the safest spot. 'Cause if they keep yelling, you gotta hope that they ain't that mad, and they'll just go away," he explained.

But they rarely did. One male staff usually wasn't enough. They needed at least two or three more. Half-hidden, Joshua listened while the men hurled their shoulders against the door. Finally, the bed frame crashed on the floor, and then the men slammed through everything else.

"What about when they find you?" My mouth went dry.

"The bunch of them start grabbing your hair and punching. You better get still when they pull off your pants and shirt. I know to stop kicking inside the seclusion room with them."

"Why's that?" I asked.

"'Cause you'll get a good stomp in the ribs," he answered matter-of-factly. "Did you want some more water, Mr. Bridge? They might get another cup if I ask." He held out his own.

"I'm okay, Joshua, thank you. Can we keep going, just for a little more?"

"I got me another secret if you won't tell," he interrupted.

"What's your secret?" Megan asked, trying to lighten the mood.

"At night, I sneak up and lean that closet door against the door to my room. When I'm asleep, they gotta hit that door first. Even under the sheets, I know they're coming." He swerved in his chair. "It looks like an accident when they bump that door, but I can get the desk light and see which ones are there."

I nodded back and promised not to tell.

"Anything else you wanna talk about?" he asked.

The boy was getting fidgety again, his eyes dancing around the room. He had given me plenty. There were dozens of others, all older than him. But I kept going.

"Joshua, do you know what Vocational Rehab and Building 112 are? An older resident brought it up."

"Vocational Rehab and Building 112 are in the same warehouse but separate. Pulling worms is in the front part. Building 112's in the back."

"What do you mean 'pulling worms'?" I asked.

"'Cause they come in them rubber chains from the factory," Joshua answered incredulously. "You gotta pull 'em apart before you bag 'em. No one cares if you take a couple for yourself."

The institution's only on-site vocational activity for children was piecework from a nearby factory that manufactured artificial fishing lures and worms. The facility then sold them to the tackle shops in town. Black and lime-colored worms seemed to be everywhere on the grounds.

"So, why would another boy want me to see the back of a warehouse?"

"Because it's like a prison with cells," he answered.

I was surprised. "How do you know that?"

As Joshua explained, the staff had shown him the cells and told him they were something he should be sure to remember. The implied threat had to be chilling.

I glanced at the table microphone. "Can you tell me more about them?"

"Yeah, there's three of 'em with a black metal door and a big lamp hanging down from the ceiling." He dished his hands together, miming the incandescent bulb.

"Do you know anyone who was left inside them?"

"Beverly," he whispered.

She had been in the cells for two days and then discharged.

He straightened up. "I don't think you'll find the cells."

"Why?"

"'Cause they covered 'em up the week before you came."

"Who did that?" I asked calmly.

"I dunno. Just ask somebody." He tugged at my notes, smiling playfully.

"What has to happen for you to leave this place?" My head was getting dull from the heat.

"I need to have two successful home visits. But first, I gotta find myself a foster home."

"What do you mean you have to find a foster home?"

"They ain't done it. They ain't doing it now. It's up to me."

"What happened to your aunt and uncle? Why can't they take you?"

"They abandoned me," the boy replied flatly.

"Where are they?" My question sounded pointed. "I mean, where do you think they could've gone?"

"I don't know, they moved." His voice was unsteady.

"Why were you sent here in the first place, Joshua?"

He took off his glasses and folded them on the long conference table. For the first time, the twelve-year-old's naked eyes stared at me. "They said it was recurrent sexual abuse from family, physical abuse, willful neglect…" His words were oddly formal, as if he were ticking them off from his chart. It was difficult to tell if he actually understood them. "Now, I have trouble with people," he continued, "trouble getting along."

The room went still while he waited for me to say something. Nothing came. I held my eyes on him, letting him know I was still there.

The boy put his glasses back on and broke the quiet for us.

"You know what I'd do," he said. "I'd find me a big bomber and drop a bomb on the whole place. Tear the place up." He stopped short. "I don't mean it really." Glancing at Megan and me, he asked, "Would you take me, the two of you?"

"Take you?" I asked. "Take you where?"

He held his eyes on mine. "I won't be bad. I promise."

Megan and I struggled for something to say. From beside the camera, she volunteered, "Mr. Bridge and I aren't married. We only work together."

Rubbing his hands against his knees anxiously, he looked across the room. "I thought I'd ask."

Back at the motel and lying on the bed, I kept thinking about Joshua's question. There was an incident that took place one afternoon at MacLaren. I could've only been there a few months. Outside the school, I spotted a line of adults and a crew of administrators leading the way. Turning to the boy playing in the dirt beside me, I asked him who they were.

He tucked his shirt into his pants, patted down his hair. He ran toward the line of them and hollered back, "They're parents."

I yelled in his direction, "Whose parents?"

He waved me toward him. "Our new parents. Maybe I'll get one."

I turned away and went back to playing alone.

Chapter Twenty-Two

MacLaren was the dumping ground where Los Angeles sent the children it had given up on. The county dubbed them the "non-placeables." MacLaren and Eufaula weren't identical, but they were close. Eufaula was the last stop for many of Alabama's children. They were the kids who foster families and group homes found too much to handle. Both places always had an open bed. And two or three phone calls were enough to get a child sent there. They were the kids, to use Ricky Wyatt's words, that the system "just got tired of."

Cut off from the outside world, MacLaren orderlies reimagined daily routines into humiliating rituals. Ward staff improvised myriad punishments, which they excused as the "natural consequence" of misbehavior or a mistake. But there was nothing natural about it. Inside those deafening walls, an orderly's whim could send a child to the corner or sit in a chair for hours on end. Time-outs drifted into entire days. That was the least of it.

To an outsider, things looked organized, controlled, and arranged. In reality, there may have been rules, but they bent to the moment. Find yourself alone with an adult and you learned what the full swipe of authority can do. Expect kindness and you were humiliated—a sharp slap across the face, a knee in the back, a stripping that went too far. And then there was the shame of punishment coming from a stranger.

Hope had her moments. A frustrated swat across my backside, flipping off the TV, taking my favorite toy. "I wouldn't do it if I didn't love you," she yelled. There was a promise in that punishment: *When we're done with this, Andy, I'll still love you.* There was no such thing in the backhand of a stranger. It was the humiliation of punishment without the guardrails of love.

Lessons came at me hard and fast in my earliest weeks at MacLaren, and like the new kid in the schoolyard, I learned the important ones from the hands of children. I stripped down with the other young boys, placing my clothes on my bed as ordered. All of us were aged five to seven. Under the lines of overhead lights, male staff paced back and forth, inspecting the naked row of us, shouting to drop our hands. Catching me covering myself, one of them yelled into the side of my head, "You think you got anything worth hiding?"

We marched single-file through the bright hallways, past the other dormitory wings, staff offices, and children's empty playrooms. Administrators and strangers walked around us. From the surrounding wards, older naked boys merged into us. The single line devolved into a mob, tumbling against the walls. The older boys shoved while the younger and smaller of us stumbled ahead.

I hesitated in front of the rows of huge tiled rooms. Water blasted from the walls while the staff tossed soap bottles at us. "Get moving, gentlemen. Get your asses going!" A few of the other young boys split beneath the spigots closest in view. I tried following, staying close, but the attendants kept shouting to walk deeper and make space for the others pushing against us.

Without knowing how, I was in the deepest recess. Behind me, I caught the faces of two or three stragglers from the original line of younger boys. The ceiling lights glistened down the wet walls, over our slick bodies. For a moment, it was only us, a handful of little boys from my ward. We waited, trying to stay clear of the water pelting us, covering ourselves with our hands, unsure what to do.

The shouts of deeper voices rolled closer. The space flooded with older teenagers, muscled and thicker than any of us. The confident bodies of young men banged against us, laughing. I heard words that I didn't know: "faggot... cocksucker... cunt." I retreated to the back corner of the shower, spigots blasting against my back.

I had seen the edges of it before, a clump of young men gathered around a younger or smaller one. That evening, the group circled me, cornering me into the deepest end, grown hands grabbing at my slippery body. I swung back, flailing my arms and hands against them. When one shoved me, I slipped on the tiled floor, while another yanked my feet up, knocking my head against the wall. I heard the laughter of grown-ups through the rows of hard tile.

The older boys circled me, grabbing and twisting between my legs. A cluster of fingers stabbed inside me and lifted me inches from the floor. A heavy foot pressed my spine against the tiles. I couldn't hear clearly. Were they yelling "Rub in"? Or was it "Rub out"? It didn't matter. One stepped over me, squatted, and pressed his anus against my mouth. I squirmed to breathe and felt a fist twist my head sharply back into place. He slid back and forth, rubbing his penis across my face, before finally leaving. Back in the dormitory, I pulled my underwear up, acting as if nothing had happened. Boys who screamed, or worse, cried, were targets for more.

Chapter Twenty-Three

I could smell Carlton's Old Spice or whatever it was. The two of us stood jammed in the basement stairwell of the boys' dormitory. He was fumbling with the key ring at his belt, flipping to find the one to open the lock. He yanked the metal door, and I slipped on the dry leaves hitting the wall. "There it is, Counselor."

Inside the small waiting area was a folding chair and a pile of *Sports Illustrated* and *Car and Driver* magazines. I glanced overhead in the earthy air.

"What do staff do here?"

"Modify children's behavior."

Carlton waited behind as I entered.

The rooms were situated halfway down the darkened corridor. Every one of them was stripped bare. A mattress lay on the floor with a gray felt blanket thrown to the side. The closets were empty, their drawers removed.

Through an open doorway, I eyed a half-eaten tray of food. The room stank of urine. A pair of boy's yellowed underwear lay balled in the corner.

"Is this B-Mod?"

"You got that from Russell, didn't ya?"

I ignored the question. Russell and Kimberly had both mentioned it. Rubbing my hand over the door frame, I looked back at Carlton's figure at the end of the hall. "Why are there no doors?"

"Why do you think?" he replied. "You need to read up on the legal definition of seclusion buried in all those years of court orders." He walked to the room closest to him, gave its entrance a good look. "It's about the door and lock."

Eufaula had found a loophole.

The definition of seclusion in the lawsuit was putting a child behind a locked door. A mental professional's written order was required if the child was to be *locked* behind that door for more than one hour. After twenty-four hours a new order was necessary. All of that would leave a paper trail of what had happened, an explanation of why a child was isolated, for how long, and where it had taken place.

Without the lock or door, so Carlton's logic went, dragging a child into the basement wasn't seclusion. It was the kind of argument that a law school professor chided me for making in class. He called it overly technical, pretzeling around the clear intent of a rule—to use his words, the whole thing was "too cute for a good lawyer to use."

I looked in the room next to me, the one with recent evidence of a child. "Do you think Russell agreed with your definition?" Without waiting for a response, I followed up, "Why is this place called B-Mod?"

"Behavioral Modification," he answered dryly.

"How long do you keep a child down here?"

"Now there's a stupid question, isn't it, Andrew?" he answered. "As inexperienced as you might be, you know well as I that I am represented by opposing counsel. Even the question without my response is highly improper, unethical. Some teacher at Harvard should have told you that rule."

Carlton had tried to intimidate me from the start, and he enjoyed it. But this time he delivered one of those ham-fisted slams that left you thinking, *Is that the best you can do?*

My actions weren't unethical, because opposing counsel didn't represent him—the lawyers for Alabama represented the lawsuit's named defendant, the State Commissioner of Mental Health, not Dr. Carlton. Court orders also gave us the right to question any staff, including him. I stared into one of the empty rooms, saying nothing. Finally, he shoved his hand against the door's crash bar and stepped out into the open air. "We're about done with this. It's time to go," he shouted. I walked past him and out of Eufaula alone.

The fate of thousands of people inside Alabama's institutions hadn't always been left to a small team of nonprofit lawyers. In March 1971, President Nixon's Justice Department joined the lawsuit at Judge Johnson's request. Federal experts traveled to southeast Alabama and toured Eufaula. At the time, local judges and state officials were dispatching dozens of children to the new facility, and as children arrived, federal experts were there to greet them. Interviewing children and reading their files, experts discovered that Eufaula's practices were stunningly similar to what was going on at Bryce Hospital.

The Department of Justice pleaded with Alabama and the court, asking for an immediate halt to Eufaula's use of an "array of punishments," including the seclusion of children for excessive periods without the approval of psychiatric professionals. Outside consultants were just as worried about restraints and seclusion. After the Nixon administration collapsed, the Justice Department's interest ebbed and flowed through subsequent presidencies. One after the other, Alabama's governors traveled to Washington. Each had one demand: end the federal government's involvement in the lawsuit. The state would find a sympathetic ear in the person of future chief justice of the Supreme Court John Roberts.

After graduating from law school in 1979, John Roberts was just getting his career started. He had already clerked for Justice William Rehnquist, and at twenty-six years old, he was now a special assistant to President Ronald Reagan's attorney general. On December 11, 1981, Roberts wrote to Attorney General William French Smith. He wanted to update his new boss that Alabama governor Fob James had stopped by the office the week before to discuss the *Wyatt* lawsuit. As Roberts put it, Governor James had discussed "specific aspects of the case" with the administration's new appointees. The governor wanted the federal government out of his psychiatric institutions, and Roberts agreed.

Choosing to title his memo "Alabama Mental Case," Roberts didn't claim that conditions at Bryce Hospital or any other facility had improved—they hadn't. Governor James had failed to implement his own plan to ensure "the safety and welfare of the patients." Nor did Roberts mention that the Justice Department's own experts had uncovered unacceptable seclusion practices and ongoing punishment of children.

The reason Roberts gave for throwing in the towel was that the fight had taken too long. He complained that the battle for patients had become "interminable," and enough effort had been spent fighting for their safety and welfare—as if the fight for justice had an expiration date.

The Justice Department drew down its challenge to Alabama, dismantling whole chunks of its defenses for adults and children in the state's mental institutions, before finally withdrawing altogether. Deprived of the federal government's vast resources, we were left to carry on the fight alone—a thinly staffed and underfunded civil rights organization.

Chapter Twenty-Four

I had been back in my office a week when three new boxes of documents arrived from Montgomery. They were the first files that Alabama's attorney general's office had produced for individual children, mingled with incident reports that described violent altercations between children and staff. Going page by page, I separated the two categories of documents.

After alphabetizing children's individual files and then searching repeatedly, I found one common group of children missing. If I had interviewed or met with a child, their particular file hadn't been included. Even the case history for Travis Moore—the boy who had read for me inside Eufaula's school—wasn't there.

In all, there weren't more than a few dozen individual children's files. Nothing near the number of children currently at Eufaula, or the others that had come and gone during the 140 weeks we had requested.

Alabama's decision to exclude these files violated the rules of court, not to mention a lawyer's ethics. But those were legal niceties compared to the immediate impact.

Children's files contained their social histories: who they were, where they came from. Why of all places had they ended up at Eufaula? Was it their first stop in Alabama's custody like Kimberly, or had the state sent them through a trail of foster homes, juvenile justice facilities, and psychiatric hospitals like Russell and Joshua? We lacked clinical notes that offered clues about children's daily lives. Putting aside the on-site interviews, those notes would be the only thing we'd get that even came close to telling us what it meant to be a child inside Eufaula.

Without those and other day-to-day accounts, we didn't know what psychotropic or other medications Eufaula prescribed children. Equally absent was what, if any, efforts staff took to manage, reevaluate, or change medications. At twelve years old, Joshua was on Thorazine, Tegretol, Ritalin, and Haldol. Kimberly was fifteen and had been given Zoloft, lorazepam, plus two others that she couldn't remember. Both children described an overflow of drugs inside the institution, enough to support an underground trade. Daily notes on how often staff administered tranquilizers on an "as-needed basis" were missing. We had little proof of when, where, and why staff put children on ward restriction or in the seclusion room, and as I learned from Carlton, the days that a child spent in the basement's "Behavioral Modification Unit" were never written down.

But most important of all, the state's lawyers knew that withholding the files of Russell, Kimberly, Joshua, and Travis meant we had no parents to call or visit. We had no way to find out why a mother and father had sent their son or daughter to Eufaula, no way to know if they had tried to get their child back and what steps they had taken.

I was halfway through the boxes when I remembered that I had promised to call the children I had met with after I left. I reached for the phone, dialing the number listed on Eufaula's marketing materials for parents. I hung up somewhere after a count of fifteen beats. I rang again. Nothing. Glancing at my watch, accounting for the one-hour time difference between Washington and Alabama, I remembered the children were at lunch. I tried again at home thinking the boys were on their wards for shower time. Nothing. For the remainder of the week, I called from home when I got up, hoping to catch a child before breakfast, from the office at alternating times throughout the day, and again from home in the evening. Nothing. Going up the chain of command, as a parent might, I tried the facility's main administrative number. After identifying myself each time, I got the same response: "Call the child's ward."

Finally, I asked for Carlton's line. Surprised when he picked up the phone, I asked to speak to Joshua. "That child is not available, Counselor."

"Then I'd like to speak to Kimberly or Travis." I glanced at my notes from Russell. "Wayne Tatum, if he's there."

"Those children are not available."

I ticked off the names of five random children from recent incident reports. Each time, Carlton answered with an exact drawl, "That child is not available."

Pausing, I asked, "Is there a time when any child will be available when I call?"

"No," Carlton replied, and hung up the phone.

I shoved aside my notes. Parents wouldn't have had any better luck reaching them either.

Alabama was doubling down. When the state's lawyers discovered that Marci White was from North Carolina and another expert was from Georgia, they sent letters to each governor, demanding a justification for their attack on a southern "Sister State." Marci refused to resign, but the expert from Georgia immediately withdrew.

From April through July, deadline after deadline passed. Alabama ignored every request for a document, declined to answer any interrogatory, objected to the deposition of hospital and state employees at whatever level. What was once the barest pretense of courtesy between the opposing parties was replaced with outright hostility.

Swamping us with nightly court filings, followed up with delays and refusals to comply with the court's orders, Alabama stuck to the promise its assistant attorney general made at Bryce Hospital: "You just keep on doing it, 'cause y'all ain't winning this time."

Alabama's institutions had coalesced into an impenetrable wall. Contrary to federal court orders, hospital administrators refused to allow our experts or attorneys to speak with patients privately. All interactions were to be monitored. After our first tour of Bryce, Brenda returned to videotape ward conditions and patient interviews. When an administrator demanded the taping stop, Brenda refused. After Brenda reminded the woman that she had the right to record conversations with our clients, a male ward nurse lunged at the camera. The two broke into a shoving match. Hearing about it, I couldn't help but laugh. Brenda won and went right on recording everything.

The authority of the court depended on the lawyers' good faith in following the judge's orders. That was the bare minimum required for the process to work. But as they'd shown for the last twenty-three years, Alabama didn't want it to work. Every evening, minutes before five o'clock, we could expect as many as a half dozen objections to come streaming across our fax machine. The practice was called "papering us," and it required days in the library researching how to counter each one. Jerry announced that he was going to ask the Department of Justice to rejoin the case, if only to force the state to start handing over discovery documents.

It was more than just documents: Alabama knew how to intimidate. There was a reason for the hostility and the staff's nervousness during our first tour of Bryce: they were scared of losing their jobs. Alabama's attorneys had pumped out thousands of letters to each state employee there and at every other institution, including Eufaula. The letters falsely warned that we were there to eliminate their jobs, and the result was a code of silence. Staff were keeping their eyes on us and each other, watching for signs of betrayal as we walked through the wards.

From the start, Bryce Hospital had always set poor against poor since the confinement and seclusion of impoverished men and women also meant employment for their fellow Alabamians who fed them, mopped the floors, and cut the grass. As Bryce expanded and other mental institutions and facilities began springing up in the poorest parts of the state, Alabama created an industry involving more than ten thousand patients and even more local jobs, as well as a bureaucracy to administer it.

Ricky Wyatt's aunt, Mildred Rawlins, who had brought the lawsuit in the first place, worked on the wards for patients over fifty years old, where there was never even a pretense of providing psychiatric care. One-quarter of those committed to the institution were elderly, confined with "no record of mental illness because there appeared to be no place else for them." As a nurse's aide, Mildred bathed, dressed, and fed the men and women who had been sent to Bryce to die. After Judge Johnson dismissed her plea to get her job back—in a footnote—she was on her own.

Among the state's delaying tactics was one that targeted me personally. The state's attorneys claimed that in my visit to Bryce with Brenda, I'd falsely claimed to be a state employee, ordering patients and staff to answer whatever questions I had. The attorneys had them ready to back what I had done, and if need be, they were willing to testify to my conduct in a federal court hearing.

The court filing included an affidavit signed by a Bryce Hospital employee. The employee wasn't the ward nurse I had met. This employee was a female nurse. According to her sworn statement, she and I had engaged in an extended conversation. She went through it point by point. I had identified a female patient who I knew was in the hospital's East Wing, Ward Five. I had insisted that the woman be woken and dragged from her bed. An orderly brought the confused patient to the visiting room, and while I left the nurse to watch, I told the patient that she could tell me anything. I explained that I was an attorney with the state and clarified that it would be a good idea for her to answer my questions. I had spoken to the woman cruelly, not caring about what she had to say. The observing employee wrote that my conduct had been so inappropriate that she had decided not to speak with any of us.

Alabama's actual attorneys hadn't bothered letting the nurse know that there was no way for me to identify any patient by name, much less where that patient happened to be housed. We had asked for that exact information from Bryce Hospital, but Alabama's lawyers had refused to hand it over. None of that mattered.

It was a complete fabrication, but the attorneys hit their mark anyway. Reading through the court filing, the accusation alone was embarrassing. Nothing like this had ever happened to any of the associates or partners that I remembered in private practice.

My head went to worst-case scenarios. If the federal judge believed the allegation, he could do as little as verbally reprimand me or as much as publish an opinion detailing my misconduct, free to be cited as precedent in this lawsuit and any other. A fuller investigation by the state bar would follow, suspending my legal license and imposing a fine. Or the decision would arrive at my disbarment and the end of the legal career I had barely started.

I tapped on Jerry's door. "Have you seen the motion for contempt against me?" Then before he could answer, I added, "You know it's not true. It's a complete lie."

Jerry looked up from his desk, evidently aware of it, countering my concern with a trace of irritation. "We'll ask them to withdraw it."

"Ask them to withdraw it? It *is* a lie," I repeated. "A lie filed in a federal court, told to a federal judge. That is sanctionable in itself."

He glanced out the window and turned back. "I'm sure it all is."

"What if they refuse to withdraw? What happens?"

"Like anything else, the judge will set a hearing for the motion to review and determine your conduct. Consider it a badge of honor. That's what they do." Jerry stared at me, offering his grizzled advice. "Toughen up."

Chapter Twenty-Five

Malcolm tossed the envelope across my desk like a Frisbee. "Looks like something personal from Andalusia, Alabama," he said. "Where the hell is that?" I thanked him and cut the envelope open. The pages had been torn from a gluey scratchpad, one of those impulse buys you find at a local pharmacy. The handwriting was thick, the language formal:

> Re: Wayne Alton Tatum (D.O.B. 4-21-81)
>
> To Whom it Concerns:
>
> I am the legal parent of Wayne Alton Tatum, and feel compelled to refresh the memories of all having any knowledge of Wayne, and his long

> running history (since 1986) of the need for appropriate Mental Health.

With that introduction, Wayne Tatum's grandmother Colleen went through the boy's history. His mother committed suicide shortly after his second birthday. After that, his father abandoned him to Colleen and her husband. This worked out for a good while, nine years in all. Until Wayne found his grandfather on the kitchen floor, crippled by a massive stroke. Struggling to care for both her husband and a child, Colleen sent Wayne to stay with another relative. The month after that, Covington County's juvenile judge sent Wayne to Eufaula.

Colleen included photocopies of Wayne's absent-minded doodles. "This is a drawing Wayne did about his mom," she went on. From the handwritten date of his birth, Wayne had drawn it on the Monday after his eleventh birthday. The year he had found his grandfather in the kitchen.

The first drawing was of an empty woman's dress, patterned with stripes and a carefully placed line of buttons. The outline of a handgun drifted overhead. The next was the backside of a pair of cowboy jeans, an object protruding out of the right hip pocket. I wasn't sure where it was all going until I got to the next sketch. Wayne drew himself standing with his left hand pointed at his head. He colored in the short sleeves. Under his crew haircut and an awkwardly drawn ear, a spot was blackened. Finishing it, Wayne put himself floating on the page, pointing his boots up and penciling lines of blood spitting from his skull.

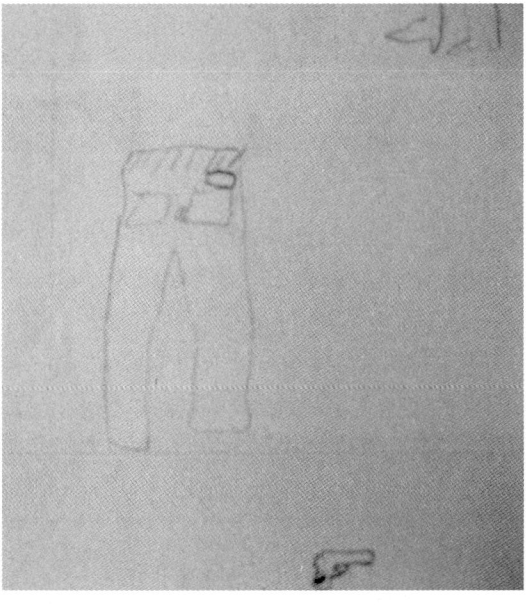

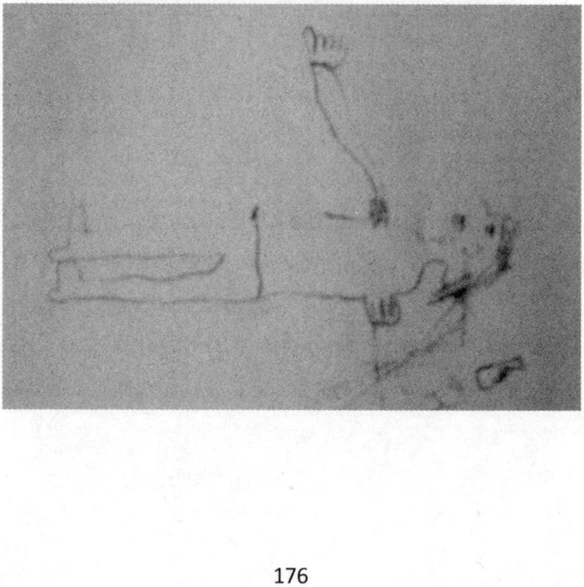

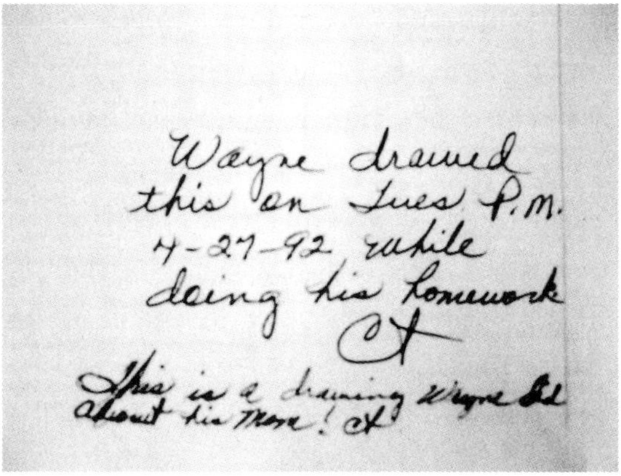
Wayne drawed
this on Tues. P.M.
4-27-92 while
doing his homework
CT
This is a drawing Wayne did
about his Mom! CT

Colleen ended the boy's last sketch with a note. "Wayne drawed this on Tues. P.M. 4-27-92," she wrote, "while doing his homework. CT." Then she added, "This is a drawing Wayne did about his Mom! CT." She made no mention of how Wayne's mother died. The drawings did it for her.

I thought of a boy doing his fifth-grade math, switching from fractions and decimals to drawing what someone had told him that his mother had done. Though here he was drawing himself. He must have imagined the details on his own. His rendering was direct and explicit. Wayne hadn't drawn them in the back of a book or on a scrap of paper that he could tuck away out of sight. He'd done it where it would be discovered—on his homework. He wanted it to be found. He wanted someone to explain why his mother had done it. If she had loved him like they said, why wasn't he enough to keep her here? I placed the note inside my desk drawer. There was nothing about it to share around the office.

At one point Brenda leaned in from the hallway. "We got good news," she said. The federal court had granted our request for a protective order. Alabama had been forced to stop sending employees letters saying we wanted them fired. Brenda smacked the doorjamb with a roll of documents. "They can kiss that crap goodbye."

But the damage was done. From ward nurses to senior administrators, nobody was about to testify against the state.

"Good news," I agreed. "Did you bring up the motion for contempt against me?"

"The state isn't withdrawing their allegation. We'll go forward with a hearing once we get it calendared."

By the onset of fall, Alabama's lawyers were winning. They were running out the clock, and we were running out of money. Jerry and Brenda were hitting up donors and private foundations, asking them to open their pockets to support a sprawling lawsuit with no end in sight. We hadn't heard a word from the Justice Department on our request to rejoin the case—but the answer was starting to look like a fat no.

The state flatly refused to provide complete records of patients, including those of children. Alabama's lawyers had contacted families and guardians, along with patients themselves, telling them that individual treatment histories weren't going anywhere. The court had warned them not to do it, but they'd gone ahead and done it away. We had a right to those records, and as Alabama knew, we desperately needed them. Left empty-handed, we couldn't argue what any specific patient had gone through. We wouldn't so much as know their name. I had heard that worry in Jerry's voice when we had first divided up which pieces of the lawsuit each of us would handle. He knew his opponents' tactics well.

Since the lawsuit's earliest days, medicating children and adults into a stupor had been common practice. We needed to know what was going on now. Was medication being used for the welfare of children—or the convenience of staff? There was clearly no justification for keeping children in a basement for "behavioral modification." And we still had to locate the cells in Building 112.

Our backs against the wall, we filed a motion for contempt and demanded sanctions against its attorneys for obstructing lawful discovery. Going after an opponent's lawyers was a big deal. It was also a gamble. Judges didn't appreciate lawyers squabbling over what the court had or hadn't ordered them to do. And even if we did win our motion, the state's attorneys wouldn't personally lose anything. With a wink and a nod, they would all be compensated from the state's coffers for any fines the court might order them to pay. The risk was worth it, though, because if we did win, the court might order Alabama to reimburse us for months of wasted time.

We spent weeks preparing for the three-day mini-trial. Jerry led the argument, swatting back interruptions from our opponents and ignoring their open disdain for the entire proceeding. We won that fight, like nearly every dispute before it. The federal judge ordered the institutions to start answering questions and handing over documents. No longer could the state refuse to turn over its most damning material: internal investigations into staff violence against children, as well as children harming themselves. It had to explain how staff were trained to physically restrain children, though by now, we knew what they were actually doing.

The judge's ruling read like a win—at least on paper. The problem was what the judge hadn't done. He hadn't ordered the state to pay us for what its attorneys had already cost us. He hadn't threatened them with future penalties if they continued their behavior. Nothing could stop them from slow-walking or ignoring every request we made for documents or other information. As we soon learned, that was precisely what Alabama planned on doing.

What we needed was the Justice Department to reenter the case. But the election of a young southern Democrat to the presidency had us worried. Bill Clinton had taken Kentucky, Tennessee, Arkansas, Louisiana, and Florida but failed to win over the deepest of the South. That meant the Justice Department's decision on whether to rejoin the lawsuit went beyond them weighing Alabama's inevitable complaints about the federal government's trampling of southern rights. Our request would be decided by the raw politics of a new president with one eye on reelection and not wanting to alienate voters.

Jerry and Brenda were running back and forth between our offices and the Justice Department. The Bazelon Center had worked on legislation for people with disabilities, and political contacts on the Hill were being called. There was the hope of a meeting with White House staff. But nothing seemed to move. The polls for Clinton's first midterm November elections weren't helping. For the president from Arkansas, a wipeout looked likely across the South. Bad news for Clinton was terrible news for us—or so we thought.

We didn't expect the president's reelection strategy to drop Alabama entirely. The state had resoundingly rejected Clinton in the 1992 presidential election, and as we approached the midterms, things hadn't gotten any better. Even Alabama's Democratic Senate candidate had taken up Clinton bashing. He won that Senate seat and, the day after the election, announced that he was now a Republican. If Alabama had anything to say to Clinton, it was "Don't bother."

After that debacle, allowing the Justice Department to rejoin the suit wasn't going to make an ounce of difference to Clinton's reelection hopes. The department agreed to assist with discovery and the adult institutions. Alabama might ignore and stonewall our small nonprofit, but those tactics wouldn't work with the Department of Justice. The weight of the federal government was behind us, and things would be different now.

Chapter Twenty-Six

When I walked into Eufaula for my next visit, two weeks had passed since the Justice Department returned to the case. Alabama's lawyers hadn't said a word about it. Megan was waiting inside the main conference room. I dialed the receptionist.

"I'd like to speak with Dr. Carlton, ma'am."

"What about?" the woman asked.

"We'd like to tour the Vocational Rehab building."

The woman said nothing.

"I'm sorry, ma'am. Did you hear me?"

"Yes, Mr. Bridge, I heard you. I'll check if he's available." Before I could respond, she hung up.

The phone rang forty-five minutes later. "Mr. Bridge, Dr. Carlton has gone for the day and won't return until tomorrow."

I checked the wall clock. "Ma'am, it's not even two in the afternoon."

From her end, a muffled conversation followed, before she returned. "I know what time it is. You'll need to wait until tomorrow."

I caught Megan's eyes. "We're giving you ten minutes. After that, we'll tour the building on our own."

Almost immediately, an unfamiliar administrator emerged from the institution's offices. He pointed at our camera. "I have a right not to be recorded."

"Not a problem," I replied, though he had no such right. Outside the conference room, I leaned into Megan. "Be sure that thing's on the moment we get close."

I hadn't noticed it driving up my first day, but the structure we were approaching was visible from the far end of the parking lot where the fencing ended near the thicket of woods. The flat-roofed warehouse was two stories high, constructed of corrugated metal and mounted to a slab of concrete about the size of a football field. Other than the heavy cabling connected to Eufaula's power lines, the building stood on its own.

At the top of the path sloping toward the building's rusted doors, our anonymous guide repeated, "I have a right not to be recorded."

Megan steadied the video camera on her shoulder. She was smiling, keeping the man in her sights.

A few steps inside the structure, I looked up at a cavernous ceiling with dangling industrial lights. A long roof stretched out overhead with, as far as I could make out, rows of more industrial fixtures lighting the distance. As Russell and Joshua had described, waist-high workbenches occupied a chunk of space a few yards away. Chains of rubber worms and insects were strewn inside several crates. Beside them lay plastic baggies stuffed with the lures children had pulled apart. I turned when Megan pushed open the door, and the administrator stepped to the side.

"Do you mind if I go ahead?" I asked. The man shrugged, and Megan held her ground behind us. "All right, I will." As I neared the workbenches, he uttered, "I haven't given you permission for anything." It was a strange remark, defensive. He was thinking about something ahead.

I made my way forward. Blocks of the interior were walled off, making it difficult to know what I was searching for, what direction to take. The walls extended to the height of the roof; small door windows to rooms were blacked out with paint. I passed an opening to what looked like a classroom. Another twenty yards or so, the warehouse opened into full width. The three of us halted at a rising wall of plywood boards. Unlike the others, this wall fell short of the ceiling. I broke from the group, rubbed the wood, and caught the smell of fresh paint on my palm.

I pointed to the far side and said, "I'd like to go through the single door over there, please." The man held his stare before reaching for his key ring. Megan fell back as he and I crossed into a second room, facing another entrance. This one was blocked with trash bags and stacks of boxes of tools and scrap wood. I turned toward him. "Are you going to let me know if we're getting near the end?" He ignored me. I waved at Megan. "Would you give a hand with that stuff piled at the door?" She set the camera on the warehouse floor. While the man watched, Megan and I began clearing a path.

I turned back as Megan lifted the camera to her shoulder. "Sir, I'm asking you to unlock this door."

Realizing Megan was behind us both, the man snapped out again, "Don't get me on camera." Before I could reply, Megan quipped back, "Don't you worry. I won't be the one to get ya." He dropped his hands to his side, refusing to move until Megan directed the camera squarely at me.

He approached the entrance, another key in hand. A few feet from me, the man looked up. He bided his time, apparently considering his options, before returning to the lock. Finally, he swung open the door.

Inside a narrow pathway were the closed doors of three prison-like cells. While the man hung behind me, I lifted the wooden crossbar from the closest cell, laid it on the earth-covered ground. I paused for a moment. The anonymous man, the damp chill, what I was about to enter—it all made me nervous. I looked into the dark window, pressed the latch pin to the side. The lock had been left unbolted.

Finally, I shoved the heavy metal door open. I stepped into the cell alone. I scanned the walls around me, the red clay floor at my feet. What looked like children's handprints were smeared across the sides, as high as they could've reached. A stench rose from the blackened corners where children had defecated. Above me, a grate topped the cell. Through that, a bright bulb burned.

This was where Eufaula's staff dragged David Dolihite, not just once but likely several times. I didn't know the dates or the full extent of what transpired. But this was where Eufaula began for me, when a woman from Harvard Law School told me about a lawsuit in Alabama, with children locked in a cage or some sort of cell.

I circled the grayish-white walls, smeared with red mud. Here was what mattered. What mattered was what happened where I stood. Whether David screamed under a dead or burning bulb, he was left here with nothing, without the people he loved and things he knew. As tightly as he held on to himself, the threat of complete abandonment must have terrified him. When Eufaula's staff retrieved him, he might have been quiet like I was when MacLaren orderlies came back for me, hauling me out of the basement room. I grew into a man and entered the world. David never got that chance.

During his first two months at Eufaula, David Dolihite had hurt himself at least six times. He was rushed to the nearby Lakeview Community Hospital emergency room on three occasions. Despite that, staff stuck with his set treatment plan. Nothing changed. He received one thirty-minute session of individual therapy and another forty-five minutes of group therapy each week. However, under Eufaula's rules, no child put in seclusion or placed on restriction was allowed to participate in therapy of any kind. That included David.

The result was simple math. While at Eufaula, David received three and a half hours of individual therapy with his social worker and six hours of group therapy. David's collective seclusions, time-outs, and dorm restrictions, not counting his undocumented incarcerations in the Behavior Modification basement and Building 112's cells, totaled 318 hours. For every hour of therapy, David spent over thirty-three hours in some form of isolation.

On Saturday, March 21, 1992, at 9:25 p.m., David threatened to cut himself with a piece of glass and warned staff that he was going to hurt himself when he got another chance. It was now three years later, and the staff had done nothing about it. Children were still trading glass and cutting on themselves. Russell and Joshua had also confirmed that. Answering David's threat, staff put him in the ward seclusion room, where he beat his head against the wall. The duty nurse called the Eufaula psychiatrist who had evaluated the boy when he had been admitted. Over the phone, the man ordered 50 mg of Vistaril, twice the dose that had been prescribed after David's first trip to the Lakeview ER. The psychiatrist did not see David, and no one called David's parents.

On Sunday evening, at around 9:30 p.m., David tore his closet door off its hinges and knocked a hole in it. Staff restricted David to the time-out room. According to Eufaula's time-out records, front-line mental health worker Allen Forte reported that David was found "trying to hang himself" five minutes later. When later asked if there was any question in his mind that he had gotten it right and that David was the boy he had found, Forte was clear: "Every fifteen minutes we have to do a check. He was in there, and I had to check him every fifteen minutes so I knew who was in there and I knew what was going on." Forte would've also remembered that it was David, because he took the boy's shirt and belt, then locked him in a seclusion room for the second time in as many days. After that, accounting for timing became important.

On the following Tuesday afternoon, at 3:30 p.m., David had a chance hallway encounter with a facility psychologist. The same man had assessed David when he was first admitted. Following a brief conversation, the psychologist asked for David's chart. He then wrote the boy "had not engaged in the self-injurious acts *for several days* [emphasis added] and it was possible he could be taken off close observation." It was the first entry he'd made in David's chart since the boy had arrived.

The decision made no sense. A mistake had been made, and David's clinical record laid it bare. The psychologist had failed to notice the entry about David's two self-injurious incidents over the weekend. But they were there, documented by Forte only a few lines above the psychologist's own notation. That careless error had left David alone, without anyone to watch him. The result was tragic.

It wasn't staff who found the Dolihite's son, forty minutes later. It was David's fourteen-year-old roommate, Eddie Weidinger. When Eddie walked into their shared room and turned to the closet, he saw David hanging from the clothes bar by a shoelace. As Eddie screamed down the hall for help, staff—along with several other boys—rushed to the room. Precautions had been taken to remove scissors, knives, and all other sharp objects from the floor, but administrators had failed to remove the wooden clothes bars from the closets. Eddie leaped to his friend, began frantically gnawing at the shoestring. Adding to the already lapsed time, more minutes passed until Eddie broke through the shoelace.

Emergency CPR was performed. David was revived and driven by ambulance three hours north to Children's of Alabama hospital in Birmingham. By the time David got there, doctors determined his functioning level to be that of a three-year-old. He had suffered severe hypoxic brain damage on his ward. David's parents were finally called.

"But when I got back to work," Forte recounted, "I was told that it wasn't David Dolihite that tried to hang himself that [Sunday] night." He continued, "I was told that I made a mistake, and what I had written down on the observation sheet here, that I needed to change because I had made a mistake. And the investigator came down from Montgomery, and I written out an affidavit saying that I had made a mistake." Pressed if he had, in fact, made that mistake, Forte replied, "No. But there's a lot of things that be swept under the rug."

A boy had hanged himself, and the authorities at Eufaula were closing ranks.

Chapter Twenty-Seven

"He was a teenage rebel without a cause," David Dolihite's father would later remark. "He would stand up for the underdog. When he got to the age of fifteen, he knew everything and was going to do everything. That's how it all started before Eufaula."

From across the coffee table in the cluttered living room, I smiled quietly at Michael Dolihite. The heavyset man tapped up his eyeglasses as he pointed to a bookcase of framed photographs, including one of his son as a toddler in his wife's lap, a palm tree studio backdrop behind them. With the two of us alone in the room, Michael turned back and gazed into the empty space.

Michael and his wife lived in the same house where they had raised their four daughters and one son. Searching through online directories, I found and called him. Fifteen years had passed since

David was first admitted to Eufaula. I told Michael I hadn't known his son but had represented children at the institution about one year after David left. I wasn't sure Mr. Dolihite would want to talk to me about what happened. But he did want to talk. He wanted to talk about what the staff at Eufaula had done and what officials in Montgomery had done to protect that staff. He wanted to talk about David.

Never an aggressive or physical boy, David was prone to ditching school and talking back. After one smart-aleck remark too many, he was suspended. Meeting with the school's principal, the Dolihites agreed to restrict David to the house until the suspension expired. The next day, after Michael and his wife left for work, the fifteen-year-old went for a walk outside, and someone reported it. David's school threatened to hold his parents in "contempt of a school order" for their son's infraction. For the Dolihite family, it was a double threat. David could be sent into Alabama's juvenile justice system. As for Michael, he worked as a custodian at the high school and could lose his job. Mom and Dad agreed to do whatever the school wanted. Administrators sent them to the Baldwin County Juvenile Court. The Dolihites didn't think they needed a lawyer.

The juvenile judge had a no-nonsense reputation. She ticked off the names of a handful of kids known for making trouble and asked David if he knew them. He answered that he had heard of them because they went to his middle school. After a fifteen-minute hearing, the judge confined David to a group home for teenage boys.

There, he proved to be an easy target. The older boys began locking him inside a closet during afternoons and weekends.

Walking home from school, he found the same boys beating a younger child. David intervened, and for that, he was sent to appear before the same juvenile judge on a charge of assault. Reviewing David's case for the second time, the judge decided that his behavior warranted a stint at Mount Meigs, the same juvenile offender facility where Carlton later sent Russell.

David survived Mount Meigs and after six weeks was sent home on probation. Less than a year after he first left, he returned to his old high school and stayed out of trouble. Five months later, with his sentence at Meigs fully served and his probation nearly over, the juvenile judge summoned David and his parents to appear. The family was surprised but assumed it was some sort of check-in. Nothing to worry about, they told themselves. They hadn't considered the state system had flagged their son as a known juvenile offender. This time, the judge informed David and his family that she was sending him to Eufaula for good measure. David's parents put off and resisted the judge's order for nearly a year while state officials tried to reassure them that it was in David's best interest.

"To us, it had been presented as a semi-resort mental health service in which the children would be allowed to continue in school, be given counseling, and learn to adapt to their peer systems," Michael commented. "We were told Eufaula had a swimming pool, horses, basketball, a football field... everything a teenager would love." Even so, Michael and his wife kept objecting. Until, that is, the woman from Eufaula told them that their son was going with or without their approval. If they agreed, David would be classified as a "voluntary admission."

"We did our best," Michael said. "We bought him new clothes and shoes for the trip, so he'd have a fresh start up there. My wife got it all packed up." He swatted his reddening eyes. "A sheriff arrived and picked him up at three thirty in the morning. They handcuffed him and took him off in the back of a squad car." Then his tone grew cold. "Just the way they do it. They come out, get them first thing. They take them to Baldwin County Jail. They stick them all in a cell. They bring all the county together, and they go at one time. From there, they transport them up by bus to Eufaula."

Eufaula administrators discouraged the Dolihites from visiting their son, advising them that they would disrupt his therapeutic progress. They missed their boy, and after two months of refusals, they called Eufaula's administrators and said they were coming up. With the institution a five-hour drive from their home, they thought to make a long weekend of it, to spend a few nights in a motel by the lake and several days with their son. They had packed and were ready for the five-hour drive when a state official called and told them that they'd better come to Children's of Alabama hospital in Birmingham instead. The Dolihites never saw Eufaula.

There was another boy, a child at Eufaula who had tried to warn the public what was going on. He wrote the state newspapers six years before David's arrival.

The *Montgomery Advertiser* published pieces of the child's letter. "I've been locked up fifty-eight hours so far... being locked up means being put in a room with nothing but a metal bench and bars over the window and door. It's not too nice of a place. I was in there two days straight and only got to come out to bath and get my cover." An adult who had been to the facility backed the child up, describing "kids looking filthy and with bewilderment in their eyes."

The paper sent a staff writer to interview Eufaula's director. The reporter noted that the director "declined a request for a list of infractions and punishments." Asked about the seclusion of children specifically, the director got defensive. "We don't view that as a punishment."

Eufaula's treatment coordinator reassured the reporter. "It's safe to say that only 1 percent are ever secluded." If that were true then, it wasn't when we arrived. Children's records revealed that at least 30 percent of all children at Eufaula had been put in seclusion, meaning that one of five patients who were secluded across the entirety of Alabama's mental health system were children at Eufaula. Worse yet, that number didn't account for children left in the basement rooms that Kimberly and Russell had described and that Carlton had called "Behavioral Modification" or "B-Mod" when he and I had walked through it. Nor did it include the cells in Building 112.

The article didn't mention if the reporter asked to speak to the child who wrote the letter or any other child at the facility. The boy's name was withheld. If the paper called the boy's parents to ask what they thought or let them know what their son wrote, that was also left out. Whatever happened to the boy brave enough to speak up was lost. The Sunday headline said it all: ALLEGATIONS OF ABUSE REVEAL PROGRAM THAT SEEMS TO WORK.

The paper shared photographs with its readers. One was a shot of the former air force barracks' front gate and another was of a small girl pulling apart fishing lures inside the vocational rehabilitation building where Building 112's cells were hidden. The others were flattering shots of staff circled by children. David would've recognized the social worker as his therapist. He would also have recognized one of the facility's top administrators because even I had seen him walking the grounds.

When Michael Dolihite and his wife arrived at Children's of Alabama in Birmingham, they wandered the corridors alone, looking for the ICU and their son. An administrator presented them with organ donor forms. David was on high-flow oxygen, with a botched tracheotomy that Eufaula's staff had performed trying to revive him. David remained in a coma for forty-five days. As Michael put it, no one from the state was there. "Nobody said anything."

Two years after David's injury, Alabama's commissioner of mental health Royce King was asked if he had seen his department's final report. "I probably have," King replied, "but I didn't read it in depth. They come across my desk and I glance at them. It would serve no purpose for me to read them in detail."

When David returned home, he was unable to walk. He was fed through a tube and could not speak. He wore a diaper. The Dolihites' medical insurance paid for the bills, after co-pays. The state of Alabama billed the Dolihites for David's ambulance from Eufaula to Children's of Alabama hospital in Birmingham.

"When we got his clothes back, none of them were his." The man's voice broke. "Everyone on the ward had taken his clothes and thrown in their old stuff. The suitcase was not the same suitcase." Also included was a $5.73 Eufaula check to compensate David for sorting fishing lures. Despite Eufaula's repeated calls that it needed to clear out its books, the Dolihites refused to cash it.

"They walked away," Michael said. "I trusted these people to take care of my son and to help him. That's all we ever wanted was some help. We tried mental health. We tried the schools. We tried preachers. We tried family counseling. We tried everything." The man paused, looked around the room back at the crowded photographs on the bookshelf. "The powers that be told us this was the best way to go." Wiping his eyes, he repeated the reassurance that state officials gave his wife and him before David left. "This is the state Department of Mental Health. They know what they're doing. They're run by pros. These people know."

Five days after David went home to Foley, his former fourteen-year-old roommate, Eddie Weidinger, walked into their ward room at Eufaula. It was a Sunday evening. Rather than a shoelace, Eddie tied an electrical cord around the closet's clothes bar, hanged himself, and died at the local hospital. Eufaula's staff finally ordered the clothes bars removed from children's closets the day after Eddie died.

As Michael Dolihite showed me to the door, his wife pulled up onto their driveway. She opened the passenger's side door, guided her son David across the front yard. Mrs. Dolihite introduced herself briefly while walking past me to the front door. Michael took his place beside their son when I reached to shake David's limp hand.

David was now thirty years old, though as his father explained, "In his mind he is still fifteen." He has recovered far better than his doctors predicted. David can dress himself, go to the bathroom, and walk around the block by himself. He works as a laundry sorter in town. It is a different life than what the family had planned. Michael and his wife had dreamed of traveling after the kids left the house and they retired.

Their son had his plans, too. When I asked if David had wanted to be something when he grew up, Michael's eyes beamed as if his son had never gone away. "David wanted to be a lawyer. He was for the down and out." He waved a proud finger at me. "He would've gone ACLU. He would've knocked half the country on its ear." Then, as quickly, his eyes went back to what they were.

"The powers that be." Michael Dolihite had said it, more than once. The quote came from the Bible, the Apostle Paul's instruction to Rome's Christians to submit to Emperor Nero's persecution and cruelty: "Let every soul be subject unto the higher powers. For there is no power but of God: The powers that be are ordained of God." Maybe Michael knew his Bible. Maybe not. For him, for his wife and daughters, the phrase came with the soft sound of submission. I had never heard it used without that inevitable shrug. That power had taken David. Faceless, arrogant, and hardened, it had hurt their son, terribly. When it finally left them alone, the Dolihites would care for that broken boy for the rest of their lives.

Chapter Twenty-Eight

Alabama blocked another one of our experts from touring an institution. Rather than hear the argument himself, the federal judge had delegated it to his magistrate. In turn, Jerry handed it to me to argue in Montgomery. Nervously waiting for the morning's proceeding to start, I was startled to see Alabama's assistant attorney general in the hearing room. Alabama had hauled in its howitzer and Jerry brought out his peashooter.

As the robed magistrate settled into place, Tom Bass began by saying that we had disrupted patients while they went through daily therapeutic regimens and that we had caused disturbances and left wards "agitated." Our experts had seen patients standing naked in the common corridors of several facilities while waiting for showers.

With unintended irony, Bass argued that the tours should be halted because we violated patient privacy and dignity. He didn't mention that privacy and dignity were rights that Judge Johnson had given patients and that Alabama had repeatedly demanded be removed. Finger pointed in my direction, he wrapped up by saying my tours of Eufaula were especially egregious and that "a senior administrator" had complained to him personally that I had "looked at him funny, several times." The room went quiet as the magistrate turned and signaled that it was my turn.

I replied that we had created as little disruption as possible, that our experts were mental health professionals, and that without the tours, we'd never be able to argue the full facts and conditions. On top of that, the court had repeatedly ruled in our favor on this issue. Then I went after my opponent's argument regarding patient privacy and dignity.

"Your Honor, a patient's right to privacy isn't *his* right," I said, nodding toward Bass. "The right doesn't belong to Alabama to assert on behalf of a patient. It's a simple point: patients are the ones who get to decide when to talk, who to talk to, and when to just walk away. As for dignity, patients shouldn't be paraded naked through hospital corridors in the first place."

The rights to privacy and dignity mattered to Judge Johnson, and they also mattered to me. During Hope's first commitment to a psychiatric institution, she slipped on a wet floor and broke her foot. The foot healed, but without a cast, she was hobbled with a balled appendage that a shoe could barely cover and left shuffling in pain. At the next institution, she developed a cavity in a molar, and there, the dentist decided to pull every tooth in her mouth. Dentures weren't allowed, and he left her gumming down her food for the rest of her life. When she was discharged from her last institution, staff sent her to live in a plywood shed. Any number of rights were violated in each instance, but all three had one thing in common: they had violated Hope's dignity.

The magistrate cocked her head. "You know, Tom, I think he's got you. The tours will continue. Patients will decide who they wish to speak to." Bass nodded dutifully. "When is your next tour planned?" the magistrate asked me.

"If he's keeping to schedule," the assistant attorney general answered for me, "the young man will be down at Eufaula tomorrow morning. One of their experts is coming next week."

The magistrate collected her papers, looked down her glasses at me. "Well, Counselor, I suggest you watch the funny looks."

Pulling into Eufaula's parking lot, I saw Megan pacing off to the side. "It looks like folks here have been busy," she said, waving me over. We gazed at a heap of shattered cinder block on a slope of cut grass just outside the fence. I knelt closer to the warm smell of jackhammered concrete. Each shard had the same light gray; I recognized the red smeared mud. "I'm guessing that would be the cells." Megan's eyes drifted along the rubble.

Carlton would have had to approve the demolition. And he likely covered his ass by calling Montgomery first. With that, he had his defense that he was only following orders and it never occurred to him that our expert hadn't yet seen the cells. Without the videotape of them, we would've had nothing to show the court. Carlton had come close to getting that.

The scrub of woods faced us from across the road. I took a splinter from the pile of rubble and threw it on the car's front seat. The reception trailer was locked. I thumped my fist against the door. While the hooded camera stared down at us, I shouted into the call box at the gate, "Is anyone there?" Finally, a woman spat back, "Who are *you*?"

"Who are *we*?" I yelled back. "We're two people with a federal court order requiring you to let us inside, now. We can call the judge if you'd like." The line went dead.

Finally, a woman arrived to open the gate. She pointed us toward the main conference room. Megan set up the camera, and I requested an interview with Wayne Alton Tatum. The woman promised to get him. I also asked to see Carlton but was told that he had taken the day off.

While Megan and I waited, twenty minutes dripped away with no sign of Wayne. Shoving back from the table, I headed out to find him myself. A few of the staff were smoking around the central courtyard. I strode past them to the boys' ward. The basement door was locked but the entrance leading upward opened. I headed upstairs and stepped onto the quiet unit.

To my left was a small lounge, with a battered sofa and a collection of chairs packed arm to arm. Across from me was the boys' shower room. Stepping inside, I caught the whiff of mildew from the three stalls and headed toward the patient rooms. Every door was open. Inspecting the first, I mulled over the contents: a pillow and an unmade mattress, a pair of jeans, and dirty underwear across the floor. Loneliness saturated the space. The walls were bare. The top desk drawer rattled with a couple of pencils, and the lowest held the ripped half of a months-old *Sports Illustrated*. Other than that, there was no clue to the boy who slept here.

Beside the nurse station, I eyed a reinforced door with an observation slat cut along the side. Peering through the scratched glass, I recognized a seclusion room. I turned and there was Wayne standing in a door frame.

"You're the lawyer from the lunchroom." His dry, frail voice echoed through the empty ward. "You wanna come in?"

Sunlight glared through thick wire mesh, making a crisscross pattern on Wayne's bed. He hopped up on it, his sneakers hanging at the edge. I noticed his collection of pens and pencils, a businessman's travel clock, a stack of stamped envelopes beside a notepad, all smartly arranged.

He dangled a knot of black worms. "I'm making myself a rope."

"That's a lot of clothes over there." I crouched beside his feet. A stockpile of shirts and pants was stacked across the closet floor. "Where'd you get them all?"

"My grandma Colleen packed 'em when I left, and she brung more since then. She's comin' to get me any day now. I'm voluntary."

"Where does she live?"

"She and Granddaddy live in Andalusia."

He shook his head. "You don't know where that one is."

"You gonna tell me?"

"Straight on south toward Pensacola. Do you know Opp, Alabama, Andrew?"

I couldn't help smiling. "I don't know that one either, Wayne."

"Andalusia's right down around Opp, that's where they got the Rattlesnake Rodeo every year." He tapped his knees. "You ever been to a Rattlesnake Rodeo?"

I hadn't. The annual rodeo awarded trophies to the hunter who had bagged the most live rattlers, with the coveted prize going to the one who held up the heaviest serpent. Depending on how cold the winter had been, up to four hundred reptiles participated in a week of slithering races and exhibitions. Festivities concluded with the coronation of the Rattlesnake Rodeo Queen and the presentation of her court.

"Granddaddy's took me twice, and we're going again this year. We got plans when he gets better from his stroke." He shrugged. "Next year, you could come."

"Wayne, why are you here alone in your room?"

"I dunno." He looked up at the mesh-lit window. "The staff woke me up in the morning, told me I was on restriction. I'm not supposed to leave my room until tonight."

Carlton knew that I wanted to talk with Wayne. He had heard me promise the boy that in the cafeteria on my first trip. I had also thrown out Wayne's name when I called from the office, asking to speak with children. Carlton knew I was coming and assumed I would want to interview Wayne, so he put him on room restriction.

I straightened up, kneed him in the ankle. "You wanna come with me and talk some more?" Before the boy answered, I signaled toward the door. The staff was still chatting outside in the courtyard. If they saw us, they didn't care.

We stepped through the conference room's double glass doors, and Megan beamed at the two of us. I showed him to his chair while Megan adjusted her tripod. Then swinging in beside him, I asked him to state his full name for the recording.

"Wayne Alton Tatum," he enunciated.

I reminded him to speak as loudly as possible and to stay in clear view of the camera lens. Wayne stood four foot three inches tall and weighed around seventy-five pounds. We needed to capture his manner and expressions. The overall impression he gave answering my questions would be evaluated. In addition to our expert, lawyers at the office were reviewing the videotapes of children as prospective witnesses at the trial.

He sprang up from where he was. "Can I say one thing first?"

"What is it?" I asked, anxious about the time.

He rubbed his blond buzz cut, looked at Megan. "I really don't like this haircut. It makes my ears look big." He pointed to my head. "You got little ears, Andrew."

Megan burst into laughter. "You're right, Andrew does have little ears."

Still reading through my notes, I asked how Kimberly was doing. Other girls doted on Wayne, but she was different. Kimberly kept to herself. Wayne didn't know the answer—only that one day it had occurred to him that she was gone.

His response threw me. I looked at the closed door leading to the interior offices—one I had never been through. We were never told where she went, and Alabama never turned over Kimberly's file.

"Thank you, Wayne." My tone deepened. "When did you first come to Eufaula?"

"Three and a half months ago. Right after my thirteenth birthday. That makes me the youngest boy here, after Joshua." Looking at him, he could've easily passed for nine or ten.

"Why did you come here?"

"I'm just too active," Wayne said, cracking his fingers against his neck. "Sometimes, I start arguing. I get mad very easily."

"Why so mad?" I asked.

"For one thing, I don't want anyone saying anything about my mother. She died when I was two."

"I'm sorry, Wayne." I said nothing about his drawings in my office desk drawer. He stared at his feet dangling over the brown carpet, moving on with his answer. "I don't like residents and staff making fun of her."

I wrote a note, worrying the camera's mic wasn't picking up his high-pitched voice. "So, now you live with your granddaddy and Colleen?"

"Yes, my paternal grandparents. My father left me with them when my mother died."

He absently pushed up his baseball shirtsleeves. Light lines laced his arms. I began counting the scars. "Did you do this before you were here?" I asked. He shook his head no, then took over the counting when I stopped. When he got to the highest and faintest, he went quiet.

I tapped at his wristwatch that I had noticed in his room. "Who gave you this?"

"It's Granddaddy's. Grandma lent it to me before I left home."

"I think you're the only boy here with a watch."

He rubbed the crystal against his pants. "I don't wear it a lot. Ain't no one gonna take it. It's my grandaddy's and mine."

I shifted topics. "What do you like to do here?"

"There isn't anything here." He swung his head to me, grinning. "Did I tell you I like music?"

"What kind of music?" I glanced at the wall clock. Time was getting short for the two-hour drive up to Birmingham, returning the rental car at the airport, then running to the gate.

"At home, I play the guitar and drums." He beat his fingers on the table's edge. "Did you know there was a huge fight here?"

"A fight? Where?"

"Down the hill after school last week."

"What happened that time?"

He pulled up the side of his shirt, exposing a red welt across his back. "Staff watched for a while, then came charging down that hill, jumped in, and started throwing everybody on the ground against the benches."

"How many kids were involved?"

"About a dozen, a few more."

"When the staff break up a fight, what do they say?"

"You mean the Black kid stuff?"

I looked over at him, confused. "What do you mean?"

"If they're really mad, they'll call the girls Black bitches. Not always, but sometimes they call the Black boys n—gers. They use bitch for the boys and the girls."

I asked him if he used those names.

He answered never, his granddaddy had taught him better. "You know, he's a plumber," he said proudly. "We ain't all racists down here." He stuck out his tongue at me, yanked up the tips of his ears like an elf.

Wayne eyed the two cups of water on the table. "If you're not going to drink those, can I have one?"

I handed him a cup. "Do you trade things here, medication?"

"Sometimes." He took a gulp of water.

"What medications do you take?"

"Ritalin and Thorazine, mostly."

"Wayne, if you're on restriction in your ward room, are you allowed to go to school?" I added for the camera, "It's Friday early afternoon."

He shook his head.

"Are you allowed to go to therapy?"

"No, restriction means restriction. Nothing else."

I hesitated over the next question, thinking of his age, weight, and height. "When I walked through your ward, I noticed the showers at the far end of the unit. Is that where you shower?" He nodded. I pressed on. "You said that you're the second youngest boy. Do you shower with the boys around your age or with the older, bigger ones?"

"It's first come, first served. It's best to wait until the older ones are done."

"What do staff do during shower time?"

"They mostly hang out in the lounges." He nervously placed his cup on the table. And I left the matter there.

I smiled. "What do you like most here?"

"The school, I guess. Most the teachers are nice. One of them brought me a book from home to read." That teacher was Jim Werner, whom I had met at the school six months earlier.

"I want to ask you something, but I want you to think on it before you tell me. I want you to promise."

He stilled himself. "I can do that. I promise."

"Since you've been at Eufaula, do you think you are better, worse, or just the same?"

At the thought of him being better or maybe just pleasing me, he bobbed his head at Megan. He took his time for the two other choices, and scooting beside me, he weighed his answer. "I'm worse," he said flatly.

The camera kept running, until I asked Megan to shut it off.

"Thank you, Wayne, for being with me. I appreciate your talking." I asked Megan to call the front office and get one of the staff to take him back. While I reached for my briefcase and notes, Wayne extended his hand.

"I'm glad you talked to me like you said. I wasn't thinking you'd come back."

Chapter Twenty-Nine

A week after Wayne's interview, my phone rang. I didn't recognize the caller.

"Are you the lawyer that videotaped my grandson?" a woman's voice scraped through the line. "This is Colleen Tatum. I am Wayne Tatum's grandmother."

Digging for a notepad and pen, I answered, "Yes, I did speak with your grandson."

The woman's breathing was strained. "I got this number from one of your business cards. They're floating all over the wards. What kind of lawyer are you, and where's the videotape going?"

Offering the same explanations that I gave Wayne, I listened as she wrote down what I said, whispering each point I made. I nervously added, "We're a team of lawyers. I'm the one assigned to—"

"The Covington County juvenile judge said it would take six weeks. He's been there going on four months," she interrupted. "He said you asked about the medications. Who approved the Thorazine?"

I didn't know for sure. The drug could be prescribed for psychosis or used "as needed" by staff to sedate a child. "Ma'am, about the Thorazine, has your grandson ever been psychotic?"

"No," she answered clearly. Wayne's sole diagnosis had been ADD. Though she took a moment to clarify that she'd also include sadness. "Did he talk about how his momma died?"

"He said that his mother had passed away. That's how I left it." I stared up at the ceiling. "But I did get your note and the drawings. Wayne says he misses you."

"He's a smart boy," she said softly. "We sent him to his first therapist when he was five, on account of what happened to his mother and his daddy leaving. We found another psychologist after that. When he was ten, his school suspended him for cursing at a teacher."

After Wayne's third suspension, the school sent the Tatums to court. It wasn't the same, but it was close to what the Dolihites had been through with David. The Tatums were issued a school order and told to appear before a local juvenile judge.

"Beyond that, Mrs. Tatum, has Wayne gotten in any other trouble?"

"No, nothing else. He got to be a handful. A handful too big for his granddaddy and me." She cleared her throat. "I wasn't sure. I said he was a twelve-year-old. Six weeks in a locked institution was too much for a little boy diagnosed with ADD. Now it's been months of—"

"I'm sorry," I interrupted, flipping through pages of handwritten notes. "Is Wayne a voluntary or involuntary child at Eufaula?"

"Wayne is voluntary. When my husband and I went to the courthouse, the judge didn't order Wayne to Eufaula. It was his *suggestion*." Colleen's tone sharpened. "As a lawyer, do you not follow a judge's suggestion when you're in his courtroom?"

"Yes, Mrs. Tatum, I do follow those suggestions."

"Now, think of it without that law degree."

Inside Covington County's courthouse, Colleen, her husband now paralyzed, and Wayne, in his Sunday best, had faced a black-robed judge on a raised bench. No one cautioned the Tatums that Eufaula administrators and state officials might never let Wayne go. Colleen believed "voluntary" meant she could return to the courthouse, walk across the white marble tiled floor, and up the generous staircase. She could stand before that judge, the man would hear her out, and she would get her grandson back. She was wrong.

"Every time I call, they say he's not ready. When they let me see him, they'll give me at most a day or two notice, *down to the hour*."

Colleen worked as a dietary supervisor at a local Andalusia hospital. No longer able to drive, she was left to find someone to take her up to Eufaula and back home and then another to check in on her husband while she was gone. Travel time alone took about five hours.

"I can't always get that done," she said.

I asked her how well Wayne handled pressure. If he were chosen to testify, could he get through it without feeling torn apart?

"He ain't afraid of anything, except about his momma. He's a good boy. I want him back. Would you mind if I wrote you again, Mr. Bridge?"

I repeated the office's address and added that she could call anytime. Then she lingered. "How long have you been a lawyer, Mr. Bridge?"

"Well, long enough to be arguing in Alabama."

"Are you married yet?" she asked.

"No, ma'am, I'm not."

Her sigh fell through the line. "I hope you never know what it's like to lose one of your own."

I ran the videotape of Wayne for Jerry and Brenda. The boy was chatty on camera, his eyes darting with eager grins. I told them that he was four feet, three inches tall. He was thirteen but looked much younger. I was sure he'd be useful in a courtroom. He was quick on his feet and intelligent. "The kid's voice hasn't changed," Brenda remarked. "There's not a trace of adolescence in him."

Before the tape played out entirely, Jerry gave the go-ahead to put him on our witness list for trial. But first, I needed to call Colleen back and get her permission. She was reluctant about a young lawyer handling it. I told her there would be senior lawyers from the office, an expert, and more lawyers from the federal Department of Justice. That wasn't enough. She was still hesitant. Finally, I went all in. "Colleen, I promise he will be okay," I insisted. "We'll get him through it. I won't let you down." She asked if she could be there in the courtroom for him. I told her that was what everyone would want. Finally, she relented.

"Okay, Andrew, go ahead."

The next step was getting ahold of Wayne. I got Alabama's counsel on the line and said I was calling my client in one hour and expected the staff to get him to the phone. I had tried reaching children using the number given to parents, and the phone rang forever. Children and families relied on the ward's pay phones, leftovers from when the facility had housed men and women in the service. This time using a pay phone had an advantage—there was no way for staff to listen in.

Sure enough, one hour later, Wayne's voice answered when I dialed the boys' ward.

"Hi, Wayne, it's Andrew."

"I know, they said you were calling." He lowered his voice. "They don't look happy."

As a boy, I went to hearings after being taken into foster care. Even with that, I had never been told to climb into a witness box and answer questions from a bunch of intimidating adults. I had never done what I was about to ask Wayne to do.

Wayne listened while I went through the basics. I would be the lawyer who started the questions. I would begin with his family, what his life in Andalusia was like, and what had brought him to Eufaula in the first place. I would move on to what had happened to him there. After that, other lawyers from the state of Alabama would have their chance. I explained that I knew them and that their questions would be harder. Much harder. Trying not to frighten him but wanting to be sure that he understood, I said they would try to confuse and trip him up using his own words. They would try to make him look like a bad kid, which I reminded him he wasn't.

Wayne hadn't said a word the whole time.

"You still there, Wayne?" I asked.

"Yeah, I'm here," he answered.

"It's your choice. Your grandma and grandpa will love you, always. No matter what you decide, you are important to me. I won't forget you."

He asked what mattered most: Would his grandma be there? I said that she would be.

"All right, Andrew, I'll do it."

"Okay, we'll do it together."

News of the trial was already making the local papers. Alabama lawyers had begun calling the local press, hoping that some harmful ink about us might pressure the judge. Jerry responded to the worst of it but mostly ignored it. After Wayne's name appeared on our witness list that was sent to Alabama's counsel and was filed with the federal court, the news of a boy coming forward about Eufaula hit the *Birmingham News*, the *Montgomery Advertiser*, and the *Tuscaloosa News*. The same papers covered the lawsuit with the first photographs of Alabama's institutions in the lawsuit's earliest days. Readers knew of the boy only as "Wayne T." or "W.A.T."

Chapter Thirty

Walking into the office the following week, I was surprised to see a wall of taped and stamped boxes. Malcolm was seated beside the phone. "There are more in the photocopy room," he said. Beside a stack of mail, he pointed to a pile of at least a dozen more. "Your buddies in Alabama sent gifts."

I cut through as much tape as I could, finally ripping several box lids in half. Inside were dozens of children's files, internal office memos, and several stacks of incident reports. Malcolm whispered into my ear, "Just amazing what a nudge from the Department of Justice can get you. Marci called. She got a set of copies, too." Malcolm was right. With Justice's reentry, Alabama's objections to our tours of institutions hadn't completely stopped, but they had slowed. The fax machine had almost gone quiet, and the stream of frivolous motions had dwindled. With the trial fast approaching, it was the calm before the storm.

Our first request for documents had gone out more than a year earlier, and why Alabama resisted for so long was now clear. Included in the haul were the internal investigations we had requested. There was the memo that Kathy Sawyer had written to Royce King pleading with him to change things at Eufaula. And there was more.

Marci and I went through the incident reports first. Eufaula accounted for only 5 to 6 percent of the state's psychiatric patients, but staff there were responsible for nearly 20 percent of abuse and neglect cases statewide. And that was only substantiated cases. As a matter of official practice, the state refused to pursue any allegation where the child and staff member were the only witnesses to what had happened. The full extent of abuse was simply unknowable—that nearly 20 percent was likely only the tip of the iceberg.

Eufaula had a fifty-acre campus, and as I had seen myself, the former radar base had countless spots where a staff person could disappear with a child for a few moments. The child's word counted for nothing. An attack? A rape? All the accused adult had to do was say the kid was lying, and the matter was dropped.

The more we read, the more it became apparent that we were dealing with serial abusers. People doing it again and again. The state knew who they were, and Eufaula's documents proved it. Twenty-one Eufaula employees had been investigated five times. Eufaula had investigated five of those same employees fifty-five different times. Not one of them was fired. Close to half of the institution's children had been abused or neglected more than once.

Eufaula had created a culture where predators thrived, and no institution in Alabama came close to Eufaula's pattern of repeated abuse. One frontline staff member, identified only as "Mr. M," had been involved in thirteen different investigations over five months. His first violent act against a child (that could be proven) occurred just after he was hired when he slammed a child's head against a wall. He was reprimanded and given a one-day suspension without pay. During the second incident, "Mr. M. teased and taunted a child, making inappropriate and unprofessional comments concerning the child's mother." In yet another episode, he called a child a "white cracker... pecker head... four-eyed bitch," then told the child to "suck my dick." Other than two warnings, Eufaula allowed Mr. M to carry on working for seven months before firing him. Of the six complaints against him for physical abuse, officials acknowledged only the first claim, the one that occurred soon after he was hired.

Every child at the facility was from a working-class or impoverished family in Alabama, and on average, they were over one hundred miles away from home. Regardless of whether they had come with a family searching for help or had arrived there from a foster home or another state placement, every child had been promised safety.

Chapter Thirty-One

Alabama prizes its courthouses. Centers of power, they convey the appearance of order and steady justice. Harper Lee set *To Kill a Mockingbird* in the Monroe County courtroom she remembered, with its white curved balcony overlooking the witness chair and jury box. The judge who sent Wayne to Eufaula did it in Covington County's courthouse, constructed of granite with a Beaux-Arts clock and Corinthian columns. Each of Alabama's sixty-seven counties had its own seat of justice; several of them could count two. Wayne had never testified before, much less been asked to represent hundreds of others, and had no idea what to expect. Ahead of us, the federal judge's bench sat empty, a navy-blue wall stippled with brass-colored stars above it.

The months of depositions and expert tours, the evaluation of patient records and internal state documents—the whole of discovery had come to an end. Even if we had been given more time, we couldn't have afforded it. We were down to our last dollars. Both sides had filed their pretrial briefs, hundreds of pages of facts and arguments.

The morning before the trial was set to start, I brought Wayne to the courthouse. I opened the door to the witness stand and led Wayne inside. "Remember, you may not enter or leave this chair until the judge gives you his permission." He took his seat to the left of the judge's bench. I stepped into the center of the courtroom. "Here, on your right, you'll see me with the other attorneys from Washington. Over there"—I pointed—"the attorneys for the state of Alabama will be watching." I held my eyes on the boy, his shoulders scarcely reaching the top of the mahogany witness box. I reminded him, "You must not lie, no matter what, whether you think it'll make me happy or upset. Even if it's hard."

"Will they hear me?" he asked.

"Yes." I smiled. "They'll have a microphone in front of you, but you'll have to lean into it as much as you can." Circling my hand at the bench, I added, "And you won't refer to the judge as 'you' but as 'Your Honor.'"

Wayne pressed, "How long will it last?"

"I don't know. We'll see tomorrow."

I escorted him back through the courthouse halls, around the metal detector into the lobby where Colleen was waiting.

"My husband and I bought these for tomorrow." She opened a shopping bag and laid out a boy's plastic-wrapped white dress shirt. There was a clip-on tie, another dress shirt, and two sets of pressed pants. "He has to dress respectfully for the judge." She flattened the bag beside Wayne's courtroom wardrobe. "I thought you'd help pick one?"

"I'm sorry, he can't wear these." I imagined the effort she had gone to—the expense—and felt bad. I looked at Wayne in his jeans and Power Rangers shirt. "I'd like him to wear what he has on now."

"Those are play clothes." She pulled Wayne's arm toward her. "And they're dirty from the bus trip."

"I want him to dress how he was when we met at the institution. I want the judge to see him that way," I responded.

Colleen looked at the lobby and security guards. I reached for the bag and slid the clothes back inside. "Could you wash what he's wearing in the hotel sink?"

"He and I can do it together." She smoothed out the front of her dress.

Within days of learning that we planned to call Wayne to testify, Alabama's officials discharged him from Eufaula, where he'd been for nine and a half months. Eufaula called Colleen, and when she excitedly asked what day she could head up and bring her grandson back home to Andalusia, the administrator corrected her. Wayne wasn't going home. He was being transferred to the state's foster system and assigned to a placement north of Birmingham in Cullman, some 225 miles away. Colleen was devastated. When the trial date approached, Alabama officials gave Colleen and her husband one week with Wayne in Andalusia. The decision to allow the one week was cynical: it would sound better if the boy answered on the stand that he was staying with his grandparents rather than in foster care.

Wayne would have to be ready, and I would have to be ready with him. Wayne didn't know it, or even Colleen for that matter, but when he arrived the next morning, he would be the first witness I had ever examined at trial.

Chapter Thirty-Two

United States district judge Myron Thompson was the second Black federal judge in Alabama. Childhood polio had left him with a limp. He had grown up in Tuskegee, gone to Yale College and Law School. Thompson had presided over the lawsuit long before I had arrived.

Judge Thompson removed his narrow set of reading glasses and peered at the opposing lawyers. "Before we begin, we have the motion for contempt against Mr. Bridge," he announced. "Is he in the court?"

I rose and noticed the journalists behind me in the gallery. With his eyes straight on Thompson, one of the private attorneys for Alabama began, "Your Honor, if it pleases the court, as the motion for contempt describes, Mr. Bridge has on multiple occasions represented himself falsely, claiming to multiple staff and patients at the state's institutions that he served as counsel for Alabama. He advised staff and patients that they were under an obligation to speak with him and answer whatever questions he had."

Replacing his glasses, Judge Thompson looked down impassively. Evidently familiar with the document, he returned to Alabama's counsel. "Your motion states you are ready to provide staff and patients to testify as to Mr. Bridge's conduct. Are you prepared to produce them?"

"No, not at this time."

"Has the state prepared affidavits in addition to the one that has been filed or other evidence to support its allegations?" Thompson asked.

"No," the lawyer replied.

"Is the state prepared to produce the Bryce employee who filed the affidavit?" Thompson was being diligent.

Again, the answer was no.

"Is Alabama prepared to withdraw the motion?"

The lawyer shook his head. "No, Alabama is not."

Thompson tapped his gavel. "Motion denied."

And that was that.

Moving quickly, the judge announced, "We will begin with the children's institution at Eufaula." He glanced at his watch. "In one hour, the gallery will be cleared for the first child's testimony."

Alabama's lawyers took their end of the outside corridor. We took ours. The elevator pinged and we gave it to them. Scurrying inside the next, we stared at the bronze floor dial. The doors opened unexpectedly.

A tall, frail white man asked if we wouldn't mind making some space. He spoke with a plain Alabama accent, something you heard on the street. His face was thinner than what I remembered from old news clippings. The dark blue business suit was the kind that a man buys with his wife, puts up with one fitting, then wears for the rest of his life. Jerry smiled. "Of course, Judge Johnson." Johnson was quiet. He had to know that the lawsuit was set for trial, but a comment would've been inappropriate.

He nodded. "It's good to see all of you." An awkward moment passed, then almost shyly, he asked, "Would you have time to stop by my office?"

Frank Johnson was now seventy-seven years old. President Jimmy Carter had elevated him to the US Court of Appeals for the Fifth Circuit. The courthouse bore his name, just around the corner from the Montgomery Greyhound bus station where a white mob had beaten and stomped a group of Freedom Riders in 1961.

Before he was elected to Congress, John Lewis was one of those Freedom Riders. He was twenty-one years old when he appeared in Frank Johnson's courtroom. Already battered by the crowd outside, the young man was nervous. Judge Johnson looked down at him from his bench and, as Lewis recalled, asked him to explain the Freedom Rides and why he wanted to head on to Mississippi. Lewis answered that he "began this ride to see how the law was carried out... and wanted to continue it for the same reason." Johnson lifted the injunction that barred the riders from continuing on, and two days later, Lewis and the others boarded a bus bound for Jackson, Mississippi. Like so many others, Lewis referred to Frank Johnson as "the real governor of Alabama."

A newspaper editor described Johnson and his family's life in those years: "Johnson was a much-hated figure among white Montgomerians, almost universally so. There was more fear than anything else: Fear of the unknown, of the customs of hundreds of years being upset. And none of the leadership in Montgomery was preparing the community for change." Fortunately for the Johnsons, they were never socialites. Their friends organized a farewell in their honor at the local country club in his hometown before he left to take up his first judicial appointment in the state capitol. The Johnsons forgot to attend. "It's hard to ostracize someone who does their own ostracizing," the judge remarked.

His paneled office was sparsely furnished, empty of plaques, proclamations, and engraved tributes. Johnson approached me and shook my hand. I wished I had said something smart. Something to impress him and let him know that I knew who he was.

Glancing around, I spotted a letter-size frame hanging from a nail. The lines had been typed, then printed out on copy paper. The quote was from *A Man for All Seasons,* the play about Sir Thomas More standing up to Henry VIII. A lawyer, More was convinced that the law was on his side and that words on paper would protect him from a monster of a king. He famously got it wrong, and Henry cut off his head.

An interviewer asked Johnson why he had stuck his neck out. He shook his head. "My oath as a United States judge requires that I decide cases like I think the law requires it be decided.... If I had been working in a steel mill, I would've done the same thing." Frank Johnson wasn't a complicated man. He put on that blue suit every morning, went out into the world and did his job.

With the bailiff's call to rise, Judge Thompson emerged from his chambers and waited for the room to quiet and all to be seated. He spoke tersely, "Are plaintiffs' counsel ready to proceed?"

I turned to the public gallery, nodded at Colleen in the front row. She wore a purple dress with white flowers. The benches around her were empty, except for our expert Marci White to the far side. With a tap under the table from Jerry and a nod from Brenda, I rose. "Your Honor, we are ready." I paused nervously. "If it pleases the court, we wish to call Wayne Alton Tatum." As we had planned, Wayne emerged from the witness room, stepping in front of me into the courtroom well. A moment of quiet passed while I reviewed my notes and questions.

From the table opposite ours, a chair scraped against the floor. Alabama's assistant attorney general rose. "Your Honor, the state discussed this matter with Mr. Bridge and informed him of our objection to the presence of the boy's grandmother in the room. We ask the court to remove Colleen Tatum."

Feet from the witness box, Wayne froze in front of Thompson. He locked his eyes on me. I had promised him that she would be there. Colleen barely noticed when I smiled at her to stay. She kept her attention on her grandson.

I lifted a hand toward Wayne, signaling him not to move. I reminded myself to keep quiet, to listen and then make my move after the opposing counsel's. Give him some rope and let him run with it.

"The boy will clearly, as he is now"—the attorney pointed at Colleen—"look to his grandmother in response to every question Mr. Bridge asks." He waited for Thompson, expecting that objection alone might be enough to expel Colleen. "Mr. Bridge knows that, clear as day."

Thompson said nothing.

Resting over his notes, the attorney then went on: "The state plans to cross-examine Mr. Tatum. The woman influences his responses, Your Honor, and removes any credibility he could possibly have. *Nothing* permits this."

At the drop of "nothing," Thompson glanced at Wayne, then the adults watching. "I remind counsel for the state of Alabama the boy is only thirteen years old, and the woman in the gallery is his grandmother." From behind his small glasses, the judge nodded at Colleen to stay, then at Wayne to climb into the witness box.

Alabama's attorney retreated to his chair.

Wayne leaned into the microphone, and his soft, amplified voice filled the courtroom, promising to tell the truth. In the same witness box where teenager Ricky Wyatt swore to tell the truth about his life at Bryce decades earlier, Wayne Tatum was ready to do the same for himself, for Russell, Kimberly, Joshua, Travis, and Ashley, and for thousands of other children who passed through Eufaula. Though he couldn't have known, he was also there for David Dolihite and his roommate Eddie Weidinger. For those who doubted how much one child's testimony could do, Wayne was about to prove them wrong.

As the room hushed, I realized I hadn't told Wayne that a courtroom cleared of reporters still held a battery of legal assistants, law and file clerks, a uniformed bailiff, and stenographer to watch, listen, and record every word he said. I feigned a smile and turned to my first page of notes.

I hadn't asked Jerry or Brenda for permission to break with court protocol the night before. It was a gamble, and I read what I had prepared verbatim. "Your Honor, before I begin my examination, I'd like to ask for your leave to conduct my questioning beside the boy at the witness box rather than where I am standing now."

Thompson turned to Wayne, seated but fidgeting. "I'll allow it, Counselor."

I crossed the well, rested my arm on the witness box, and dipped the microphone closer to the boy.

"Wayne, this is a big room. A lot's going on here, a lot of people, so I want you to do your best to relax." The boy nodded. "Also when I ask you questions, I'd appreciate it if you'd answer as directly as you can. If it's a yes or no, please say your answer rather than shake or nod your head." Like I had told him, Wayne held still without interrupting. "Finally, if you want to take a break, have a rest or glass of water, let me know, and I can ask the judge."

I pressed my hand against my notes. "Would you tell us your full name?"

"Wayne Alton Tatum."

"Where are you from, Wayne?" He glanced at me, confused whether I meant the foster home where the state had transferred him after Eufaula or his grandparents' house, where the state had allowed him to stay for the week before the trial. "Where were you born, Wayne?"

He smiled, relieved. "Andalusia, Alabama."

"You are now thirteen years old?" Wayne nodded. I corrected him to answer verbally. "Yes, sir."

"Where do you live now?"

"I live in Cullman with a foster family." He looked at Colleen across the room.

I took another breath, preparing to go deeper. "Wayne, I'd like to take you through a short history of your family."

He nodded, giving me permission.

"Wayne, when you were two years old, your mother died?"

The assistant attorney general rose again, dropping his hands across his paper and files. "Your Honor," the man spoke leisurely, "counsel continues to lead Mr. Tatum. Nothing he's doing is allowable, much less of any value."

"The Federal Rules of Evidence, I believe, allow me to lead during direct when the witness is a child." I held my breath beside the witness box.

Without addressing either of us, Thompson looked up. "Allowed."

"Wayne, your mother died?"

"Correct." He turned to the sunlit windows. "My mother committed suicide and shot herself with a handgun."

I bit the inside of my mouth, aware that it was the first time he had said it to me and the strangers watching him. We couldn't go for a break yet, too early. I gave him a moment. "I'm sorry, Wayne."

Closing my eyes, I cleared my throat. "Wayne, following your mother's suicide, what happened to your father?"

"He left." Wayne missed the microphone.

"Your father left you?" I repeated louder.

"Yes, sir." He pointed across the courtroom to the gallery. "He left me with my grandma and granddaddy. That's when they adopted me."

Colleen turned to the state's attorneys and threw them a solid nod.

"But another thing happened when you were eleven years old. What was that?"

"I come home and found my granddaddy on the kitchen floor." He pushed back in the witness chair. "He had a stroke."

"Were you the only one at home?" I bent the microphone harder to his mouth, waved at him to inch up to me.

Gripping the armrest, he struggled to reach the box's edge. "At the time, yes."

"After your mother died, was it your grandfather who was closest to you?"

"Correct," Wayne repeated.

Before entering Eufaula, Wayne had come home from school in the fall of sixth grade to find his grandfather sprawled glassy-eyed on the floor. The stroke left the man paralyzed, barely able to speak. With that, Wayne's trips to Rattlesnake Rodeos in Opp and fishing outings to the Conecuh River ended, as did his grandfather's reminders to speak his mind but never threaten, to not forget his momma had loved him and his daddy loved him still. An event that left the three hanging on together, while a boy's sorrow turned to anger.

"When you found your grandfather, how did you feel?"

"Suicidal."

"And after that, you were admitted to Eufaula?"

"Yes."

I nodded at him, letting him know we were done with the hardest first few questions. Trying to give him something to hold on to, I added, "We all know your grandmother and grandfather love you very much."

He smiled. "I know that, Andrew."

I retrieved the second set of notes, and crossing the courtroom well, I looked up. "Wayne, did anyone ever threaten you while you were at Eufaula?"

"Yes, sir."

"Would you tell me who?"

"Staff," he answered hesitantly.

"Which staff?"

"Mr. Wright, Mr. Taylor, and Mr. Powell." He turned to Thompson and clarified, "They work the boys' ward. They had a riot down the hill beside the fence where the residents go after school. The staff slammed and slugged four other boy residents and one of the girls."

Alabama's assistant attorney general tapped his forefinger against his chin, glowering. His two colleagues huddled in whispers. Our side held their eyes straight on Wayne.

Judge Thompson turned and asked Wayne directly, "And then what happened?"

"Mr. Powell picked me up by my neck, yanked me up by the hood on my shirt, carried me over the back of his shoulder to a security car, and threw me on top of the hood."

"He did what?" Thompson tilted his head.

"Threw me on the top of the hood of the car."

Thompson dipped back into his chair. "Go ahead."

"Mr. Powell and Mr. Wright came back to my room after showers. They told me if I told anyone about what happened, about them hitting the residents, that they was going to hurt me."

"If you told who, Wayne?" I interjected.

Again, he hesitated.

"Told whom?" the judge asked.

"Mr. Bridge." Wayne looked at me and pointed his finger at Marci seated at the courtroom's far side. "They didn't want Mr. Bridge and the expert lady to know."

"Your Honor, with the permission of the court, I'd like to ask Wayne to leave the witness box, stand in the well, and demonstrate what"—I wavered for the right words—"type of restraints Eufaula staff use on children."

Thompson replied firmly, "I'll allow that."

Wayne climbed down. I dropped my hands on his shoulders, angled him toward Thompson. The bailiff took a step closer, and I went back to the microphone. "Wayne, would you show us what you remember?"

Thompson peered down at the boy.

"Mr. Powell grabbed my hair." Wayne yanked at his head. "He pulled my arm back like this." He twisted his hand behind his back to his shoulder blades. "He choked me from behind." The boy wrapped his arm into a hammerlock around his throat and described staff choking children against walls. Then he hesitated for permission to continue, and I nodded. "Mr. Wright walked up to another boy resident, punched him below his neck, flipped him around, then kneed him in the back and slammed his face on the ground."

"Thank you, Counsel," Thompson remarked to me. "The witness will resume the stand."

Wayne stepped around the stenographer, opened the witness box, and climbed back inside.

Waiting for the room's attention, I scanned my prepared questions uncertain where to go next. "Did you see other serious fights at Eufaula?" I thought of Russell's neck and the hand-marked bruise that was left on it. "Russell, there was another one with Russell. Eufaula sent him to Meigs." As quickly as I said it, my shoulders slumped.

"Objection!" the assistant attorney general yelled. I glanced to the floor, embarrassed and knowing what was coming. "Facts not in evidence," the man followed up. I knew every file from Eufaula. I had labeled and ordered every document. I understood what had been asked and answered in pretrial depositions and interrogatories. However, I only knew Russell had been sent to Mount Meigs because I had seen it myself. It was a rookie mistake: I was an attorney who just offered his *own* fact, a piece of information that wasn't in the pretrial record that was boxed alongside the room and hadn't come from Wayne's testimony. "Withdrawn," I shot back. I looked up at Thompson, flushed that he let the error pass without a word.

I restated the question. "Wayne, were there any other serious fights?"

"They have chairs in the gym," he began, "and the staff sat and watched the fight like it was a TV show. Russell and the other boy were bleeding. When one of the boys stopped getting up from the floor, the staff finally got up from the bleachers."

That wasn't a surprise. Eufaula's internal reports confirmed staff instigated children to beat up others, sometimes using racial slurs to egg them on. Children reported staff would "just not get up very fast" when fights broke out between children that the staff disliked.

Thompson whispered to one of his law clerks, and the young woman passed him a document. Lifting his glasses, he bent to read it.

I returned to my notes. "Wayne, have you hurt yourself at Eufaula?"

"Yes, Andrew, but it wasn't only me."

"Would you show us, please?"

While Thompson carried on reading something, Wayne raised his pant leg and exposed a burnt welt on the side of his calf. I lifted Wayne's high top, propping up his leg on the half wall beside me.

"Your Honor." I leaned into the microphone. "Wayne is still speaking." The stenographer halted at the sound of me chiding a federal judge for being distracted.

Thompson was jolted. Brenda dropped her head to the floor. "I'm sorry," the judge remarked. He rose in his robes, leaned over the width of his bench toward Wayne beneath him. "What is that?"

Tugging his pant leg tighter and twisting in the cramped witness box, Wayne looked up. "It's a pitchfork that an older boy burnt into my leg."

Thompson looked confused and leaned closer. "Is that a tattoo?"

"No, it's what he burned on me with a guitar string."

"You purposely did that?" Thompson pressed.

"Yes, sir."

The judge stared at burn lines across the boy's puny calf. "Were you making a design or..."

Wayne interjected, deepening his voice. "No, it's a gang."

Straining to hear him, Thompson misspoke. "It was a game?"

"No, it's a *gang*." Following the court rules, Wayne corrected himself. "A gang, Your *Honor*."

With a last good look, Thompson straightened back into his chair.

To the quiet audience, Wayne detailed Eufaula's gang-induction ceremony. He named the older boy who "ruled over him" and sent him and other children on "missions," ranging from chores on the grounds to physical or sexual assault.

"Have you hurt yourself in any other way?" I continued.

"I knotted both of my shoelaces together, made a noose for my neck. I climbed on the desk and looped it through the ceiling light. I jumped down, but the light part crashed on the floor." Twisting his thumb, he volunteered the name of a girl resident that we both knew. She had cut her wrists and throat and was lucky to survive.

Wayne went on to Joshua, attempting suicide three times. He described how Joshua blockaded his ward room with everything he could find, because he was frightened of staff coming after him.

"When they got the barricade down, he was up there on the string coughing." Wayne gazed at Colleen. "I mean, Joshua wasn't fully choked, but he was coughing because he couldn't breathe, and they cut him down." He cleared his throat.

I shifted to Eufaula's use of seclusion.

Wayne described ward staff taking him to Building 112. In perfect detail, he went through the three cells, the grated windows and bulbs overhead. He gave the names of the staff who took him there, telling him to remember them. They had done the same with Joshua.

"Does the boys' unit have a basement?"

"Yes."

"Were you put in that basement?"

"I have been in B-Mod several times."

"Would you explain to the court the meaning of B-Mod?"

"It's rooms in a basement where they leave you. Behavioral Modification."

"What's the longest time you have been in there?"

Wayne gave it a thought. "About four days."

"Were other children ever put in B-Mod?"

Wayne ticked off four other boys, including Joshua and Russell. Knowing he'd made his point, he stopped. "Everybody at Eufaula has been in B-Mod."

Alabama's lawyers had argued in their trial brief that with the doors removed, children's confinement in B-Mod was merely "time-out." Put under oath, Carlton finally admitted that children were locked inside the boys' dormitory basement for up to five days. Our argument had described the obvious: the basement qualified as seclusion requiring a professional's written approval. Eufaula's loophole had suddenly closed.

"Wayne, did you run away from Eufaula?"

"Yes," he replied.

Wayne had dragged himself through a rip in the fence surrounding Eufaula, then made a run for the wire grass and piney woods. Determined to make it back to his grandparents, he bolted in the direction of Andalusia, one hundred miles away.

"How did they find you?"

"Dogs. They bit at the back of me." He yanked at his shirt collar. "They dragged me to the ground."

There it was: proof that Eufaula's staff and administrators relied on prison dogs to hunt down child runaways, borrowed from the Ventress Correctional Facility for adult men, twenty miles away. Trained to do more than only track human beings, the dogs cornered and pinned children like escaped convicts. During intense questioning in a pretrial deposition, Eufaula's patient advocate, Randy Hanklin, who had reassured children that they were free to check out of Eufaula at any time, admitted to Eufaula's use of prison-trained dogs but refused to condemn it.

About to finish, I paused. "When you think about Eufaula now, what do you think?"

"In my words?"

"Yes, in your words."

"When I heard about it, they said it was like this summer camp. That's what this lady told me after my grandma called her on the telephone. She said Eufaula had horses and horseback riding, bicycles. There was a twelve-foot-deep swimming pool." Wayne shrugged, recalling all Eufaula had was a concrete hole with stagnant water.

I lifted my notes and looked at Thompson. "Thank you, Wayne. That will be all, Your Honor."

Thompson turned to his clerk, then the bailiff. "Does the state still wish to question the witness?"

"Yes, Your Honor, we do," the assistant attorney general replied.

"We'll take an hour break." Thompson tapped his gavel. "The witness may step down."

Wayne passed me and fell into Colleen's arms. Beside the courtroom's gallery, I knelt to him. "Thank you, Wayne. You did a good job." I preferred to spend the break prepping Wayne for

Alabama's cross-examination, but the thirteen-year-old looked exhausted. Colleen wanted to have lunch alone with him. "That's not a problem," I said. "Just remember the time."

After the room emptied, I straightened several boxes of files before walking out of the courthouse. I ambled down a side street, past a group of lawyers to the Court Square Fountain at the base of Dexter Avenue. I was good at being alone. It was something I learned from Mom when it was just her and me. Somewhere along the line it became a habit. At the former slave market, I leaned against the fountain's railing and gazed down the wide, empty street that sloped up Goat Hill.

Along the rows of shuttered store windows, I took the fifteen-minute walk to the domed state capitol, past the slab marble marker commemorating where Jefferson Davis took his oath of office, then strode the street with his inaugural parade. At the base of the capitol steps, I halted at Davis's life-size bronze figure lording over the route he took, his topcoat draped on his shoulders like a Roman senator's toga, his goatee and cadaverous cheeks cast below his unflinching stare. I looked up at the square clock perched at the rotunda's base, realizing I ought to start heading back.

With a bit more time, I crossed the street to the courthouse, circling round to the back, whispering what I'd asked Wayne, hoping I'd gotten it right. Looking down at my feet, I heard footsteps behind me.

Without his robe, wearing a suit and tie, Judge Thompson smiled. "You did a good job in there, young man."

Chapter Thirty-Three

Alabama left it to one of its hired lawyers to do the cross-examination. He was the same attorney who had asked Marci White if it was possible for a child at Eufaula to consent to her rape by a staff member in a bathroom stall.

Addressing the seventy-five-pound witness as Mr. Tatum, the man covered the same ground I had, asking Wayne about his grandmother and grandfather, forcing him to repeat what he remembered about his mother's suicide and his father's abandonment. It was cruel and unnecessary. And he was just getting started.

"Isn't it true, Mr. Tatum, you have been seeing psychiatrists, psychologists, and therapists since you were five years old?" His attack was out in the open now.

"Yes, my grandma and granddaddy sent me."

"And you continued to require psychiatric treatment up to the month your grandparents had you admitted to Eufaula?"

Having trouble with the question, Wayne glanced at me.

I smiled back, closed-lipped.

"My granddaddy and grandma said I should," he repeated.

"The witness's answer is nonresponsive," the attorney said to Thompson.

The judge turned. "I remind you to question the witness in a manner that a thirteen-year-old can understand, to give him enough time to consider his response."

The lawyer scanned his notes. Pulling a thin file from a stack of documents, he returned to Wayne. "Mr. Tatum, did you see a psychiatrist in the month before you went to Eufaula?"

Wayne was barely audible, even with the microphone. "Yes, I think so."

"Are you receiving psychiatric treatment now?"

"I have a doctor I talk to."

"You have been in trouble at school, Mr. Tatum, haven't you?" As Wayne moved to answer, the man interrupted, "As a matter of fact, you were suspended as far back as the fourth grade."

"Yes, I think I remember that," Wayne replied.

"You think you remember? While at Eufaula ..." The attorney opened the file in front of him, "According to your case plan, which I have here, you have been involved in multiple incidents. Isn't that correct?"

I rose to object, to inform Thompson of our repeated requests for Wayne's history, all of which the state ignored. Jerry gripped his hand on my thigh. "Let him keep going with it," he said. I did as I was told.

"Isn't it correct that you have been involved in incidents at Eufaula?"

"Yes," Wayne answered nervously.

The lawyer shook his head. "Yes? Is that it, Mr. Tatum?"

With no cue from me, Wayne replied, "Yes, I'm sorry that's all."

"Well, I'm not sure that is all." He flipped a page. "Don't you actually hold the record for incidents involving residents at the facility?"

At that, the barely visible boy answered back in his southern drawl, "The record for all residents? That's a bunch of bull, I mean, sir."

Someone in the gallery cleared his throat, stifling a laugh. The room waited for the lawyer's reply. Face down, he reached for a second folder, then mumbled, "I have no further questions."

I rose. "I have no redirect examination."

Hearing Thompson's call to step down with a break in proceedings to follow, Wayne opened the door of the mahogany stand and crossed the courtroom to the attorneys' table where I waited. I wrapped my arms around him, and he pressed into my side.

Wayne had testified for just over three hours. He kept his promise not to lie. For all of the arguments over documents and interrogatories, the briefs, motions, and orders, and the months-long preparation for trial, it took one brave and scrawny boy to tell the truth and to lay Eufaula bare. Not a single adult from Eufaula, not one from its dozens of staff or administrators, had come forward to tell the truth.

Rounding the plaintiffs' table, I escorted Colleen and Wayne into the outside corridor and down the courthouse's limestone steps. Malcolm had booked them an extra night at the Riverfront

Inn, in case Wayne's testimony was delayed or went on for more than a day. Wayne was ready to get back to the room. Colleen had promised him his pick of movies. Before that, though, they were headed back to the capitol building. They'd missed the visitors' hours the day before, and Colleen was insisting that he get a look at the murals that wrapped up the gold- and plum-colored dome.

While the cab idled in the street, I bent to tell Wayne that I was proud, that he did well, made a difference. He shook my hand, anxious to get going. I thanked Colleen. With the two of them secured in the back seat, I gently closed the door.

Chapter Thirty-Four

It took one kid in a Power Rangers shirt to bring down the state of Alabama. It wasn't quite David and Goliath, but it was close. Judge Thompson was so moved by Wayne's testimony that he ruled on Eufaula first despite more than a dozen other institutions across the state and the thousands of men and women suffering inside them. This was where outrage met justice. Thompson's statement that the lawsuit represented "a trail of broken promises" made that clear. Now the world would know where the children lived, and how. They would know that the old military-style barracks were spartan and outdated, that the remote location made it almost impossible for families like the Tatums and the Dolihites to visit. The viciousness of staff, now made vivid, would not fade. The deliberate destruction of childhood would not be blotted out by time. All of it would be condemned. What Alabama had done would be written into history.

Thompson cut straight into the heart of Eufaula: "In theory, it was a treatment facility; but, in reality, it was essentially a penal institution." Filled with grief, Michael Dolihite had said as much when his son came home after weeks in a coma. Eufaula was just a children's prison.

Alone inside a witness box, Wayne had described the cracking of children's heads against the pavement. He explained the basement where staff had left him for days and the empty cells they had shown him as a threat. Wayne hadn't flinched when the state's attorneys cross-examined him. He defended the children that he knew—that we both knew. They were children like him, who had bravely told me their secrets and honored me with their trust. Wayne dared to tell a room filled with strangers what had happened to him and how it had all started.

With that, he had cleared the way to the only conclusion that there truly was. "After two decades," Judge Thompson wrote, "it is therefore evident that the defendants do not always follow through on a promise."

Following up on Wayne's testimony, a second child had been called to the stand. She was older than Wayne and left Eufaula before he arrived. Her family placed her in a private psychiatric facility for clinical depression. When the money ran out, she was admitted as a "voluntary patient." As with Kimberly, Eufaula informed her that she could sign herself out anytime. When she tried, the staff told her they'd have a court order committing her before she made it home. She described male gang members forcing her and other girls to do sexual acts. In thirty separate affidavits, children later confirmed her and Wayne's testimony of widespread gang activity.

"The staff know there are gangs here," one girl wrote, "and that there is gang violence here but they do nothing about it.... They know a lot of fights that happen here are because of the gangs but they still don't do anything to try to stop the gangs." Summing it up, she added, "It is not a safe place here."

State officials dismissed it as headline-seeking sensationalism, refusing "on principle" to investigate the matter any further. Eufaula did order children to stop throwing gang signs and wearing gang colors. Like everything, staff backed it up with a threat: any child caught breaking the new rule would be sent to Mount Meigs. The result was that children denied that gangs existed at all, and their activity was driven further underground.

The majority of children at Eufaula were put there voluntarily by parents who had made the mistake of trusting that the facility would protect their children. Alabama used that voluntary status as a legal defense. As the argument went, parents had placed their children at Eufaula freely, and in doing so surrendered their children's right to safety. To be blunt, put your child there and you got what you got. Alabama lost that argument flat out.

Thompson confirmed what families across the state could have told him. Once their child walked inside Eufaula's gate, voluntary status became a fiction. He wrote:

> To be at an institution voluntarily means that the child may leave the institution if he or she wants.... Children at the [Eufaula] Center may not simply check themselves out.... Additionally,

> many of the voluntarily committed children have been told that they must either voluntarily go to the Center or go to a youth corrections facility.... These patients are not in any real sense free to leave, in that they are free only to leave to go to jail.

Judge Thompson exposed the lie that was Eufaula.

I didn't know it at the time, but somewhere in all my nervous questioning, Michael Dolihite and his wife had slipped into the gallery. If I'd known they were there, I would have asked more about the promises that Alabama had made. I would have found a reason to say David's name. I had included their son in the trial brief I'd drafted for Eufaula. I had also written about his roommate, Eddie Weidinger—the boy who hanged himself and died on the same closet crossbar where David had tried to kill himself. As best I knew, the Weidingers never came to the trial, but wherever they were, I regret not reminding the courtroom that there had also been a fourteen-year-old boy whose name was Eddie. And I regret not mentioning David.

The state's largest institution for children exposed how weak decency became in the face of absolute power. Secreted from the outside world, unchecked authority bent individual conscience and overcame right and wrong. Given a sanctuary, cruelty became accepted practice.

All of it had started with Bryce Hospital. Ironically, Bryce's founder, Dr. Peter Bryce, had warned about the seduction of power that was left to itself. Confessing to a colleague, Bryce said, "In the use of power the best of men can rarely be trusted. I know by experience that I cannot trust myself to act always 'judiciously' in the exercise of absolute authority." A century later, he would've recognized what was happening inside Eufaula.

Alabama would not surrender its authority over children and families easily, and Thompson challenged its arrogance directly. "Unless serious problems are brought out into the open before the court and public, it is likely that the defendants will not address them . . . . Absent direct and continuing judicial oversight, it is likely that the defendants will not remedy a serious problem, even once brought out into the open; they will often deny it without adequate inquiry." Alabama could not be trusted with the truth.

The court ordered the state of Alabama to take immediate action to ensure the safety and protection of every child at Eufaula. Recognizing that Alabama would not act on its own, Thompson imposed an independent monitor to verify and report back on what steps state officials took. Even with that, Thompson knew that his power was isolated and weak. His authority depended on the state officials respecting what he had decided and faithfully executing his ruling. He didn't have a police force to rescue a child at the moment it was needed. Like any judge, he was left with only a bailiff to keep order in his courtroom. For that reason, Thompson placed his faith in children's parents.

He ordered the state to send letters to families, asking them to monitor practices at the institution, visiting it personally and frequently "without fear of reprisal." For one year, Alabama would be required to send that letter and the court's opinion to the parents of all Eufaula children. One month after Thompson's orders, the state announced it had halted its admissions of new children to the facility. Nine months later, with fewer than ten children left, Eufaula closed.

Wayne and I spoke three or four times after his testimony in Montgomery. When he turned fourteen, he called to tell me that foster care officials were moving him to a group home. It was then that I finally told him that I had spent eleven years in foster care. He brought up Colleen, and I mentioned my grandma Caroline. We talked about college. I said that he had plenty of time. I felt him searching for an older brother again. MacLaren didn't come up. I left it out. Big brothers aren't supposed to be vulnerable.

After that, Wayne wrote that he was being moved to a larger group home. He promised that he would do his best to behave, keep to the rules, and make it back home to Andalusia. He turned seventeen and child welfare officials transferred him "several more times." His newest placement was an "Attention Home," Alabama's term for a juvenile delinquency facility. Like Russell, Wayne went from foster care to the mental health system before being sent to the state's last stop, its juvenile justice department. Eufaula might have been shuttered, but the systemic flaws that had allowed it to exist in the first place hadn't disappeared, and kids were still finding themselves trapped in a cycle of incarceration.

I left messages for him and sent notes. If he got them, he never responded. I never heard from him while he was in state care. Officials informed Colleen that she was too infirm to handle Wayne; they also never offered her the help to do it.

From early adolescence into young adulthood, Wayne slept in state beds across the length and width of Alabama in places with names like Eufaula, Charter Woods, Thomasville, Pathway, Gateway, APSE Center, The Bridge, Sheriffs Youth Ranch, Andalusia Memorial, Brewer-Porch, Attention Homes, Methodist Children's Home, and others. He passed through secured and unsecured facilities, boot camps and psychiatric hospitals, foster families and residential treatment centers, short-term, long-term, and transitional living campuses, wilderness programs and training schools, and therapeutic and nontherapeutic group homes. Wayne was a smart kid and, at one point, did his homework and got himself admitted to the Alabama School of Mathematics and Science. The state changed his placement and forced him to leave the school.

His thickening case file muddled through the Alabama Department of Mental Health, which had kept him at Eufaula, to the Alabama Department of Human Resources, which handed him to foster care, to the Alabama Department of Youth Services, which threw him over to juvenile detention. By age eighteen, Wayne had been moved more than forty times, averaging a new placement every six weeks. When I spoke with James Tucker, he could barely keep up with where Wayne was in the swirl of changing facilities, foster homes, social workers, and schools. Five years after the trial in Montgomery, he left state care with a ninth-grade education, a GED, and finally, a bus ticket home to Andalusia.

The next time I saw Wayne, we met at the G. K. Fountain Correctional Facility in Atmore, Alabama, one of Alabama's oldest penitentiaries. Apparently, he had walked into a laundromat, armed with what he said was a BB gun that looked only like a black pistol. Explaining that he was hungry and apologizing to the owner, he handed her a ziplock baggie. She asked him if he was joking. He said he wasn't and walked out with a handful of bills and change.

Wayne appeared before the county judge who had sentenced him for a prior offense—his first. It was the same judge that recommended Wayne be sent to Eufaula. On the advice of his state-assigned counsel, Wayne entered a plea of guilty without the prosecutor agreeing to recommend a sentence. Courthouse lawyers shorthand it as a "blind plea"—one where the defendant throws himself entirely on the judge's mercy. Wayne was sentenced to twenty-one years and returned to the custody of the state that had been responsible for him since he was twelve years old.

The state of Alabama Department of Corrections released Wayne Tatum on January 6, 2023. He served the entirety of his sentence and was forty-one years old. When we spoke, he had moved back to Andalusia. His hometown had changed a lot, but he had found good-paying work. He said he was going to church and was still hoping to raise a family.

Officials declined to investigate any individual staff or administrator implicated in the abuse of any child at Eufaula. No one was fired. No charges were filed. Even after the last child was discharged and Eufaula was empty, Alabama continued to employ and pay the state salaries of its remaining 138 staff. The institution operated in the home district of Representative Jimmy Clark. Clark had been the City of Eufaula's mayor and was serving an unprecedented third term as Speaker of Alabama's House of Representatives.

Clark was known for "old, hard-ball, good-old-boy politics." He had always defended the children's mental institution and was keen on keeping its jobs. Speaking to reporters after the federal court's ruling, Alabama's top mental health appointee and lead defendant in the lawsuit, department commissioner Emmett Poundstone, announced the desire "to remain on good terms" with the House Speaker.

Officials had regularly transferred individual children from Eufaula to another one of the state's bureaucracies, pushing those children outside the lawsuit's reach. They had done it to Russell, the boy from Ensley who carried around a creased photograph of his mother in his pocket. The afternoon after we met, he left the mental institution at Eufaula for the juvenile corrections compound at Mount Meigs, then disappeared into that bureaucracy.

After losing the lawsuit, Commissioner Poundstone went even further and handed over the entirety of Eufaula's property to the Department of Youth Services, Alabama's juvenile justice system. Outside the lawsuit's jurisdiction, the Eufaula Adolescent Center reopened as a medium-security juvenile delinquency facility for ninety new children. Local jobs were saved, and Poundstone kept Jimmy Clark happy.

Chapter Thirty-Five

After I had Mom moved from her first group home and the Maricopa County sheriff's deputies came for her, she never left that second one. The place was smaller, a single ranch-style house in a Phoenix suburb. Five other residents lived there, all with serious mental illness. She preferred to stay in her room, and as much as I tried, she never wanted to take a walk or even rest in the backyard. I introduced her to my husband, Scott, and she seemed to like him.

Our visits together were quiet. I learned to keep questions to yes and no answers. Did she like her room and was the soap she used all right? There were brief moments when who she had once been reappeared. I brought her a purse and makeup for her birthday, and gazing at them on her bed, she commented that the nail polish and lipstick didn't match. I smiled at the memory of the young mother who would've made the same remark and the boy who would've made the same mistake. A childhood lasts forever.

I was in Boston attending the college graduation of Scott's oldest son when the group home director called. Rushing to Logan Airport, I didn't make it back in time. Mom died on May 8, 2022. We took her back to Colorado, and I asked Scott's sister, Laurie, if she would fly in from California to give Mom's eulogy. I scheduled the graveside service for 10:00 a.m., and typical of me, we got there fifteen minutes early. Other than staff from the funeral home, there were only the three of us, so I asked if we could get things started.

While Scott and I listened on a barren bluff overlooking the plains, Laurie opened her notes and began reading from the Book of Job from the Old Testament. Then out of the blue, a white Toyota raced up the road toward us in a hail of dust. An older man and woman slipped in behind us, whispering their apologies for not arriving earlier. Laurie went back to her Bible and then finished. I asked for a moment alone, then kissed Mom's casket and told her I had brought her home.

Pacing back toward the strangers, I noticed Scott and Laurie were grinning. Our guests were husband and wife; she was my second cousin, once removed. They had driven up from Colorado Springs after reading the announcement in a local paper the previous day. They insisted on touring me around, going from plot to plot, explaining names and how they related to me in some distant way. The woman got her mother on her cell phone and told her that Hope was in the right row under the only tree. I turned for a last look at the mahogany casket resting in the sun, and a few feet away, the woman leaned into Scott and said, "You know, we wanted to do something. We didn't know who took that little boy."

I wrote the obituary for the *New York Times*:

> Hope Rice died on Mother's Day morning at the Banner Desert Medical Center in Mesa, Arizona. She was 79 years old.
>
> Born on September 2, 1942, Hope grew up in Grand Junction, Colorado. Her parents were Caroline Gingras and Albert Rice. Caroline sold make-up door-to-door. Albert was a ranch hand. Hope's younger brother Terry served as a private in the United States Army.
>
> Hope attended the Page Beauty School in North Hollywood, California. She worked as a hairdresser, a job she loved. She was a Midwest girl, in the best sense, decent, brave, beautiful and kind. Life demanded forgiveness and she gave it.
>
> Hope leaves behind a heartbroken son Andy Bridge, who even as a man, will always be her boy.

After the lawsuit in Alabama, I returned to Los Angeles and found a new position as CEO of a children's legal services non-profit. Shortly after I started, the *Los Angeles Times* ran a story about me coming back to the foster care system that I had grown up in. What I had told the reporter about MacLaren was vague. I was placed there after being taken from my mom, was held there for a year, and was hurt occasionally. There was not a word about the basement that I was kept in, no mention of the showers where

I was attacked. As careful as I had been with the details, reading the story embarrassed me.

The following week, MacLaren's director called me. The derelict polio hospital that became MacLaren Hall had been torn down, she promised. Could she give me a tour? The new MacLaren was a two-story brick compound built six years after I had left. A wall of prefabricated concrete ran the length and width of the property, replacing the chain-link fence with barbed wire that I remembered. The youngest children slept in freestanding rectangular units. Someone had come up with the idea to call them cottages. Walking through them, I noticed the carved wood signs over the doors—PIXIES for girls, TIGERS for boys.

Now the director was calling me again about a holiday pageant. The children were performing, and she was sure that I would want to be there. It was all short notice, but she had left word with the county's higher-ups. The *Los Angeles Times* was expected, plus the *Los Angeles Daily News,* the paper that covered the San Fernando Valley. "Wasn't that where you had lived with your mom?" she asked. Hollywood stars were now showing up at the facility; autographed headshots hung in her office. She glossed through the Beverly Hills volunteers that were decorating the gym and the children who were rehearsing each day. That was when she added having me say something would be fun for everyone. I could talk about what I remembered. The new kid in town could meet some locals, she joked. I tried to come up with an excuse—an early trip out of town or a meeting that I had postponed and now couldn't avoid. But I said yes. Yes, I'd be there.

I got there early. The parking lot had been freshly tarred, the unmarred black tender enough to suck at my heels. It was the smell of travel, the oilfields on the way to LAX. Heading for the swinging doors, I passed the top-heavy junipers flaring over the sidewalk like flags in the December heat. The security guard flipped open the visitors log, and I jotted down my name. Under reason for visit, I wrote "invited." An escort was required to take me past the reinforced doors to the gym, so I waited. Carloads of guests funneled inside. Purses were searched, a few briefcases opened. Cameras were taken and held for safekeeping. Finally, enough of us had arrived to warrant radioing a second guard.

While strangers took the place of parents inside the gym, I went for the plates of store-bought cookies and the plastic bowl of Hawaiian Punch. By now, the gym was teeming. The director was lucky. The newspapers had shown up. She introduced her boss, then the LA mayor's wife. Both gave a friendly wave from their seat. She thanked several others in the audience for their work. When my turn came to stand in front of them, I regretted that I hadn't prepared. My remarks weren't memorable, something about Christmas and MacLaren's kids giving us this gift. I returned to my seat amid scattered applause, relieved that my part was over.

The loudspeaker crackled, a record scraped, and "Jingle Bells" rang through the room. The volume was quickly adjusted. A puddle of light spilled over the stage. Step by step, children's figures appeared. Not children, not exactly. Just tiny figures completely obscured behind child-sized cardboard cutouts spray-painted in holiday silver. Awkwardly, the kids grasped their paper silhouettes and stumbled blindly to find their spots on the stage. They were blocked from seeing us as much as we were barred from seeing them. It was comical and frightening. The last children were still wandering in front of us when a staff member crossed and positioned each little body into place. Their faceless voices, struggling to be heard, caught up with the lyrics. I looked up at the afternoon sun streaming through the ceiling-high windows, then down at my hands and finally my shoes. I could guess what it was, the decision of a bureaucrat managing children's lives and bent on protecting the children's anonymity, keeping them safely hidden while in plain sight. In spite of it, the children finished what they had practiced and what they had been told to do.

As the show was ending, I slipped out without the guard to escort me. I walked down the block out of view, and though Mom wouldn't have liked it, I cried on the sidewalk. Not for anything in particular, only for what I knew. Everything that I remembered, and everything that had been lost.

THE END

Afterword

The Los Angeles grand jury investigated MacLaren in 2001. Children there were increasingly older, and many were psychologically and emotionally troubled. Inside the facility, an average of six serious incidents involving a child were reported daily. MacLaren had a range of policies and procedures related to reporting those incidents, including allegations of abuse by staff against children. However, the grand jury found a four-year backlog of investigating those incidents. Investigations of MacLaren's staff were conducted by their coworkers and were characterized as "perfunctory at best." Multiple employees were discovered to have previously undisclosed criminal backgrounds.

Los Angeles County continued to operate MacLaren for another three decades after I left. Thousands of children passed through it. Appearing before the board of supervisors, I argued for an independent investigator to be placed on-site at the facility. The supervisors refused. I asked for MacLaren to be closed, and I wasn't alone. Child advocates, lawyers, and community members asked Los Angeles County to stop placing children there. The supervisors knew that Los Angeles had sent me to MacLaren as a boy. I never mentioned my sexual assault there.

In one instance, the supervisor whose district included MacLaren called my boss, Eli Broad. Mr. Broad was a major philanthropist in Los Angeles County. Across from her desk, she demanded that I apologize for publicly stating that MacLaren be shut down. Mom never liked bullies, and my response to the woman was a polite no.

MacLaren was shut down in 2003. Los Angeles County finally did it, in response to a class-action lawsuit that alleged that staff had physically abused dozens of children and had routinely failed to care for children with mental illnesses and behavioral disabilities. I didn't participate in the lawsuit. Part of me still wishes that I had, though it would have been too much and too close.

The story of MacLaren continues to unfold. On September 19, 2022, the state of California extended the time for claims against childhood sexual assault. Hundreds of MacLaren survivors have come forward, describing sexual assaults at the hands of staff and other children—assaults that go as far back as the 1960s. The lawsuits have only begun to wind through the courts.

Congress recently acted to restrict the placement of children in institutional settings like MacLaren and Eufaula. The Family First Prevention Services Act became law in February 2018 and was the most sweeping reform for foster children in decades. According to the American Academy of Pediatrics and Chapin Hall at the

University of Chicago, these reforms came "after decades of advocates and youth with lived expertise raising significant concerns about systemic abuse and mistreatment that was happening" in many children's facilities across the United States.

Dozens of national organizations have supported the legislation, including the American Academy of Pediatrics, American Psychological Association, Children's Home Society of America, Children's Defense Fund, Foster Care Alumni of America, FosterClub, National Association of Counsel for Children, National Association of Social Workers, National Court Appointed Special Advocates, National Child Abuse Coalition, National Foster Parent Association, North American Council on Adoptable Children, and Prevent Child Abuse America.

Outside the reach of these reforms is the "troubled teen industry." Against their will, tens of thousands of children are sent to residential treatment centers across the country. These facilities are an array of wilderness programs, boot camps, behavior-modification facilities, and religious treatment courses, all of them promising to make a child better. What it amounts to is big business. Many are for-profit organizations with facilities across multiple states. They operate with no federal oversight and collect billions of dollars for their owners. News investigations and children's accounts continue to uncover excessive seclusion and restraint, overuse of psychiatric medications, no mental health treatment, and physical and sexual abuse.

Notes

Chapter Three

1. *Valley News*, Classifieds, "Page Beauty School, 11212 Magnolia, North Hollywood," November 24, 1967.
2. *The Los Angeles Times*, "Sister Kenny Attends Polio Hospital Opening," August 25, 1950.
3. *The Los Angeles Times*, "New MacLaren Hall to House Juvenile Wards, Sister Kenny Polio Hospital Being Converted by Probation Department," November 6, 1960.
4. Los Angeles County Grand Jury Final Report 1960, p. 28; Los Angeles County Grand Jury Final Report 1961, pp. 36, 69, 71; Los Angeles County Grand Jury Final Report 1964, p. 59; Los Angeles County Grand Jury Final Rcport 1965, pp. 52, 54; Los Angclcs County Grand Jury Final Report 1966, p. 91; Los Angeles County Grand Jury Final Report 1970, pp. 42, 53.
5. *Daily News-Post* (Monrovia, California), "County to Build New Facility Next Year, MacLaren Hall: Home for Children Who Have No Other Place to Live," June 29, 1970.

6. *The Los Angeles Times,* "Trauma Is Taken Out of Tragedy," March 20, 1966.
7. *The Los Angeles Times,* "MacLaren Hall Bond Issue Will Be Put on Ballot," July 23, 1969.

Chapter Four

8. *Ledger-Enquirer,* "Mental Health Agency Known for Hiring Political Cronies," August 12, 1996; *The Selma Times-Journal,* "Mental Health Known for Hiring Cronies," August 12, 1996.
9. Evaluation of Tours, Document and Record Reviews at the Eufaula Adolescent Center, Corrected Version, Marci White, April 25, 1995 (Redacted), quoting Memorandum to Royce King, Commissioner of the Department of Mental Health, from Kathy Sawyer, Director of Central Office Advocacy, February 10, 1992.
10. *Dolihite v. Videon,* 847 F.Supp. 918 (March 21, 1994), Deposition of the Commissioner of the Department of Mental Health Royce King.
11. *Birmingham Post-Herald,* "Opponents Say James Rewarding Supporters with Jobs," September 18, 1998; *The Selma Times-Journal,* "James Friends and Supporters Getting State Mental Health Jobs," September 18, 1998.

Chapter Five

12. *One Hundred Years of Progress & Caring,* Arizona State Hospital Annual Report, FY 1986–1987.
13. *Arnold v. Dept. of Health Services,* 160 Ariz. 593 (1989).
14. Advisory Annual Report Calendar Year 1992, Arizona State Hospital Annual Report, FY 1986–1987.

Chapter Six

15. Evaluation of Tours, Document and Record Reviews at the Eufaula Adolescent Center, Corrected Version, Marci White, April 25, 1995 (Redacted).
16. Time Structured Individually Based Levels Program (TSIC), Eufaula Clinical Services Policy and Procedure Manual.

Chapter Eight

17. *Wyatt v. Stickney,* 325 F.Supp. 781 (March 12, 1971).
18. The State of Alabama did build the Mary Starke Harper Geriatric Psychiatry Center in 1996. The facility provided inpatient psychiatric services for citizens aged sixty-five and older throughout the state; *Mary Starke Harper Geriatric Psychiatry Center Family and Patient Handbook,* Alabama Department of Mental Health, p. 2.
19. *Alabama Journal,* "Eufaula Center: No Gray Areas," November 10, 1975; *The Columbus Ledger,* "Center Due Expansion at Eufaula," April 3, 1973.
20. *The Montgomery Advertiser,* "'Police State?' Controversy Clings to Eufaula Center," November 9, 1975.

Chapter Nine

21. *Birmingham Post-Herald,* "Center Helps Mental Patients Go Home," July 5, 1972.
22. *Wyatt v. Stickney,* 325 F.Supp. 781 (March 12, 1971).
23. *The Legacy of Wyatt, The Road to Self-Determination—the Past, the Present, the Future,* Alabama Department of Mental Health & Mental Retardation, 2003–2004 Annual Report, pp. 5, 11.
24. *Wyatt v. Stickney,* 334 F.Supp. 1341 (December 10, 1971).
25. Author's Interview of Ricky Wyatt and his mother, February 26, 2007.
26. In *Rouse v. Cameron,* 373 F.2d 451 (D.C. Cir. 1966), Judge David Bazelon, for whom the Bazelon Center is named, had ruled that there was a "right to treatment" for people confined in mental institutions. Bazelon's ruling was impactful; however, he relied on a District of Columbia statute, not the United States Constitution.
27. *Time Magazine,* "The Law, New Right to Treatment," April 5, 1971.
28. *The Tuscaloosa News,* "Surprise Visit Gets Results at Bryce Unit," August 3, 1971.
29. *The Tuscaloosa News,* "Partlow Conditions Deplored," August 6, 1971.
30. Alabama Building Commission, Photographs No Dates Given, Bryce Hospital: Tuscaloosa (#1–#20), Searcy Hospital, Mount Vernon (#25–#36), Partlow Hospital, Tuscaloosa (#53–#57), circa 1940, Courtesy of Alabama Department of Archives and History.
31. *The Los Angeles Times,* "Alabama Hospital—A Concentration Camp," October 18, 1971.

32. *The Tuscaloosa News*, "Bryce Work Is Pressed," August 2, 1971.
33. "*Wyatt v. Stickney*: A Landmark Decision," Lauren Wilson Carr, Alabama Disabilities Advocacy Program, July 2004.
34. *Taming the Storm, The Life and Times of Frank Johnson, Jr. and the South's Fight over Civil Rights*, Jack Bass, Anchor Books, Copyright 1993, pp. 266, 289.
35. *The Politics of Rage*, Second Edition, Dan T. Carter, Louisiana State University Press, Copyright 1995, p. 103.
36. Alabama Governor (George Wallace), Administrative Files, Mental Health, Memorandum: Legal Status of *Wyatt vs. Stickney* Now Pending in the United States District Court for the Middle District of Alabama, dated January 6, 1972, Courtesy of Alabama Department of Archives and History.
37. *The Tuscaloosa News*, "Mental Health Board Set Staff Ratios," April 19, 1972; *The Montgomery Advertiser*, "Wallace Calls Mental Health Order 'Impossible Burden'," April 25, 1972; *The Montgomery Advertiser*, "Wallace Fails to Discuss Major Issues with the Press," April 25, 1972.
38. *The Tuscaloosa News*, "Mental Hospitals Order Could Affect Campaign," reprinted from *The Montgomery Advertiser*, April 18, 1972.
39. George Wallace for President 1972 Campaign Brochure: "A GREAT LEADER FOR AMERICA"...'A Man Who Will Lead America to New Greatness.'"
40. *The Montgomery Advertiser*, Editorial Board, "A Qualified Correction," April 20, 1972.
41. *New York State Ass'n for Retarded Children, Inc. v. Carey*, 409 F.Supp. 606 (E.D.NY. 1976); *Davis v. Watkins*, 384 F.Supp 1196 (N.D. Ohio 1974); *Eckerhart v. Hensley*, 475 F.Supp. 908 (W.D. Mo 1979); *Welsch v. Likins*, 373 F.Supp 487 (D. Minn. 1974); *Horacek v. Exon*, 357 F.Supp. 71 (D. Neb. 1973); *Walters v. Western State Hospital*, Ft. Supply Oklahoma 864 F.2nd 695 (10th Cir. 1988); 233 S.E 2nd (Sup. Ct West V. 1977); *Halderman v. Pennhurst State School & Hospital*, 446 F.Supp. 1295 (E.D. Pa. 1978).
42. *Wyatt v. Stickney*, 344 F.Supp 373, Appendix A Minimal Constitutional Standards for Adequate Treatment of the Mentally Ill (April 13, 1972).

Chapter Eleven

43. Second Annual Report of the Superintendent of Alabama Insane Hospital, From October 20, 1861 to October 20, 1862.

44. Annual Report of the Officers of the Alabama Insane Hospital at Tuscaloosa, For the Year 1862 (Montgomery, Ala.: Montgomery Advertiser Book and Job Office 1862), Courtesy of Alabama Department of Archives and History, pp. 8–11, 29.
45. Bryce Hospital for the Insane, Alabama Hall of Fame 1968, Courtesy of Alabama Department of Archives and History.
46. "Survival at the Alabama Insane Hospital, 1861–1862," Bill L. Weaver, *Journal of the History of Medicine and Allied Sciences*, Vol. 51, 1996, pp. 6–7, 8, 23–28.
47. Acts of the Legislature and By-Laws for the Erection, Organization, and Government of the Alabama Insane Hospital at Tuscaloosa, Chapter XII (Tuscaloosa, Printed at the Observer Book & Job Office 1861), Courtesy of Alabama Department of Archives and History.
48. "Country Boys Make the Best Nurses: Nursing the Insane in Alabama, 1861–1910," John S. Hughes, *Journal of the History of Medicine and Allied Sciences*, Vol. 29, 1994, pp. 79–85, 93.
49. "The Evolution of Restraint in American Psychiatry," Danilo Alejandro Rojas-Velasquez, Yale Medicine Thesis Digital Library, School of Medicine, January 2017.
50. "Labeling and Treating Black Mental Illness in Alabama, 1861–1910," John S. Hughes, *The Journal of Southern History*, Vol. 58, No. 3, August 1993, pp. 435, 440–441.
51. *The Letters of a Victorian Madwoman*, edited by John S. Hughes, University of South Carolina Press, Copyright 1993, pp. 31–32.
52. Reports on the Legislative Investigation of the Alabama Insane Hospitals in 1907, Testimony of F.E. Anthony, session at Birmingham, August 29, 1907, Courtesy of Alabama Department of Archives and History.
53. Reports on the Legislative Investigation of the Alabama Insane Hospitals in 1907, Testimony of V.B. Winters, session at Tuscaloosa, September 2, 1907, Courtesy of Alabama Department of Archives and History.
54. *The Tuscaloosa News*, "Commission to Be Appointed by the Governor," July 25, 1907; *The Montgomery Advertiser*, "Market for Cotton," July 24, 1907.
55. *The Clark County Democrat*, "The Military Reservation at Mount Vernon ... Is to Be Converted into a Colored Insane Hospital," February 15, 1900.

56. An Epidemic of Acute Pellagra, George H. Searcy, M.D., Transactions of the Medical Association of the State of Alabama, 1907, p. 387.
57. Reports on the Legislative Investigation of the Alabama Insane Hospitals in 1907, Testimony of A.M. Jenkins, session at Birmingham, August 30, 1907, Courtesy of Alabama Department of Archives and History.
58. Reports on the Legislative Investigation of the Alabama Insane Hospitals in 1907, Testimony of M.E. Thomas, session at Tuscaloosa, September 2, 1907, Courtesy of Alabama Department of Archives and History.
59. Reports on the Legislative Investigation of the Alabama Insane Hospitals in 1907, Testimony of J.D. Nabers, session at Birmingham, August 29, 1907, Courtesy of Alabama Department of Archives and History.
60. *The Birmingham News*, "Asylum Investigation Being Conducted Here," July 20, 1907.
61. *The Montgomery Advertiser*, "Praise for the Asylum, Few Cases of Violence, Hospital Investigators Report," September 8, 1907.
62. *The Birmingham News*, "No Indictments in Asylum Cases, Tuscaloosa County Grand Jury Makes Report and Adjourns, Investigated the Matter Fully," September 16, 1907.

Chapter Twelve

63. *Wyatt v. Hanan*, Plaintiffs' Pretrial Brief (Corrected), Civil Action No. 3195-N, United States District Court for the Middle District of Alabama Northern Division, Civil Action No. 3195, March 7, 1995, p. 274.
64. Reports on the Legislative Investigation of the Alabama Insane Hospitals in 1907, Courtesy of Alabama Department of Archives and History.
65. *The Letters of a Victorian Madwoman*, edited by John S. Hughes, University of South Carolina Press, Copyright 1993.
66. "Modern Psychosurgery before Egas Moniz: A Tribute to Gottlieb Burckhardt," Sunil Manjaila, M.D., Setti Rengachary, M.D., Andrew Xavier, M.D., Brandon Parker, B.A., and Murali Guthikonda, M.D., *Journal of Neurosurgery*, July 2008.
67. *Encyclopedia of Asylum Therapeutics, 1750–1950s*, Mary de Young, MacFarland & Company, Inc., Copyright 2015, pp. 287–292.

68. "Gottlieb Burckhardt and Egas Moniz—Two Beginnings of Psychosurgery," Zbigniew Kotowicz, *Gesnerus,* Vol. 62, 2005, pp. 77–101.
69. "A Brief Reflection on the Not-So-Brief History of the Lobotomy," Michael A. Gallea, *British Columbia Medical Journal,* Vol. 59, No. 6, July–August 2017, pp. 302–304.
70. "Controversial Psychosurgery Resulted in the Nobel Prize," The Nobel Prize in Physiology or Medicine 1949, Bengt Jansson, thenobelprize.org.
71. *The Evening Star,* "Brain Operation by DC Doctors Aids Mental Ills," November 20, 1936.
72. *The Lobotomist,* Jack El-Hai, John Wiley & Sons, Copyright 2005, pp. 33–72, 157, 253, 342, 372.
73. *Washington Evening Star,* "Brain Operation by DC Doctors Aids Mental Ills," November 20, 1936.
74. *American Experience,* "The Lobotomist," Program Transcript, Interview of Walter Freeman III, WGBH Educational Foundation, Copyright, 2008.
75. "Psychosurgery, Ethics, and Media: A History of Walter Freeman and the Lobotomy, James P. Caruso, BS and Jason P. Sheehan, MD, PhD, *Neurosurgical Focus,* Vol. 43, No. 3, 2017, p. E6.
76. *Last Resort: Psychosurgery and the Limits of Medicine: Psychosurgery and the Limits of Medicine* (Cambridge Studies in the History of Medicine), Jack Pressman, Cambridge University Press, August 8, 2002, p. 338.
77. *The Des Moines Register,* "Lobotomy Is Aid in Relief of Depression," July 28, 1947; *Spokane Daily Chronicle,* "Brain Surgery Helps Clear Up Mental Cases," August 8, 1947; *The Indianapolis Star,* "That Body of Yours," July 28, 1947; *The Miami News,* "Results Obtained by Removing Frontal Lobes of Brain," July 28, 1947; *The Bergen Evening Record,* "That Body of Yours," August 18, 1947.
78. *Alabama Journal,* "Icepick Brain Surgery Aired at Parley," April 5, 1950.
79. *The Shreveport Journal,* "Pain Relief by Brain Operations Related," May 2, 1947; *The St. Louis Star and Times,* "Brain Operation Is Found to Relieve Pain of All Kinds," May 2, 1947; *The Phenix-Girard Journal,* "Urge Pain Operation for Those with Incurable Pain," January 23, 1948; *Chicago Daily Tribune,* "Brain Surgery Successful in Relief of Pain: Suffering by Cancer Patients Eased," April 19, 1947.

80. "Portrayal of the Lobotomy in the Popular Press 1935–1960," Gretchen J. Diefenbach, Donald Diefenbach, Alan Baumeister, and Mark West, *Journal of the History of Neurosciences*, Vol. 8, No. 1, p. 67.
81. "Godfather of the Lobotomy: Egas Moniz," Jack El-Hai, June 26, 2012.
82. "Magic Bullets for Mental Disorders: The Emergence of the Concept of an 'Antipsychotic' Drug," Joanna Moncrieff, *Journal of the History of the Neurosciences*, Vol. 22, No. 1, 2013, pp. 30–46.
83. *The Lincoln Star*, "New Drugs for Mentally Ill Tested at State Hospital Here," June 19, 1955; *The Scranton Tribune*, "Lifting of Mental Haze, New Miracle Drugs Reducing Population of 'Violent Wards," May 16, 1955; *The Akron Beacon Journal*, "Thorazine Use Wide, Effective, Doctors Tell of Good Results," June 8, 1955.
84. "History of Psychopharmacology," Joel T. Braslow and Stephen R. Marder, *Annual Review of Clinical Psychology*, Vol. 15, 2019, pp. 25–50.
85. "Chlorpromazine and the Psychopharmacologic Revolution," Michael M. Rosenbloom, MD, *JAMA*, Vol. 287, No. 14, 2002, pp. 1860–1861.
86. Johns Spoor Broome, Institutional Repository, Recording of Walter Dryfoos (Camarillo State Mental Hospital Employee) Oral History.

Chapter Thirteen

87. *Wyatt v. Hanan*, Plaintiffs' Pretrial Brief (Corrected), Civil Action No. 3195-N, United States District Court for the Middle District of Alabama Northern Division, Civil Action No. 3195, March 7, 1995, pp. 241, 257, 260, 264–270, 274, 295, 296–297.
88. *Wyatt v. Rogers*, 985 F.Supp. 1356 (M.D. Ala. 1997).
89. Johns Spoor Broome, Institutional Repository, Recording of Nancy Petry (Camarillo State Mental Hospital Employee) Oral History.
90. Johns Spoor Broome, Institutional Repository, Recording of Walter Dryfoos (Camarillo State Mental Hospital Employee) Oral History.
91. Johns Spoor Broome, Institutional Repository, Camarillo State Mental Hospital Images, https://repository.library.csuci.edu/handle/10139/5462.
92. *The Los Angeles Times*, "Huge New Red-tiled 'City' Rises for $6,000,000 Mental Hospital," February 26, 1936.
93. Grand Jury Report, County of Ventura, January 12, 1977.
94. *The Los Angeles Times*, "Deaths Investigated at State Mental Hospital," October 12, 1976.

Chapter Fourteen

95. Author's Interview of Ricky Wyatt and his mother, February 26, 2007.
96. *From Courtroom to Clinic: Legal Cases that Changed Mental Health Treatment,* Peter Ash, Cambridge University Press, Copyright 2019, pp. 7–8.
97. *The Alabama Journal,* "Former Bryce Official Says Two Court Orders Have Improved Commitment Procedures," February 26, 1982.
98. *Wyatt v. Stickney*: A Landmark Decision, Lauren Wilson Carr, Alabama Disabilities Advocacy Program, July 2004.
99. Alabama Governor (George Wallace), Administrative Files, Mental Health, Synopsis of Board Actions, 11-18-65 through 9-18-69, notation 12-22-66, Courtesy of Alabama Department of Archives and History.
100. *Wyatt v. Stickney,* 334 F.Supp. 1341 (December 10, 1971).
101. *Wyatt v. Aderholt,* US Court of Appeals, Fifth Circuit, 1972, Brief of Amici Curiae, United States of America, American Psychological Association, American Orthopsychiatric Association, American Civil Liberties Union, American Association on Mental Deficiency, National Association for Mental Health, and National Association for Retarded Children.
102. *The New York Times,* "Ricky Wyatt, 57, Dies; Plaintiff in Landmark Mental Care Suit," November 3, 2011.

Chapter Fifteen

103. *The Tuscaloosa News,* "Bryce Job Gets Emergency Funds," August 3, 1971.
104. Alabama Governor (George Wallace), Administrative Files, Mental Health, Synopsis of Board Actions, 11-18-65 through 9-18-69, notation 9-18-69, Courtesy of Alabama Department of Archives and History.
105. *The Montgomery Advertiser,* "Mental Health Units Fund Request Tabled," April 20, 1973.
106. *Dolihite v. Videon,* 847 F.Supp. 918 (March 21, 1994).
107. *Dolihite v. Maughon by and through Videon,* 74 F.3d 1027 (January 23, 1996).
108. Evaluation of Tours, Document and Record Reviews at the Eufaula Adolescent Center, Corrected Version, Marci White, April 25, 1995 (Redacted).

109. Achenbach System of Empirically-Based Assessment, ASEBA Subsequent Developments, https://aseba.org/aseba-subsequent-developments/.
110. Author's Interview of Michael Dolihite, March 7, 2007.

Chapter Sixteen

111. Evaluation of Tours, Document, and Record Reviews at the Eufaula Adolescent Center, Corrected Version, Marci White, April 25, 1995 (Redacted).

Chapter Eighteen

112. Author's Interview of Kimberly Leslie Marks, *Wyatt v. Poundstone,* 892 F.Supp 1410 (July 11, 1995).

Chapter Nineteen

113. *Wyatt v. Poundstone,* 892 F.Supp 1410 (July 11, 1995).
114. Evaluation of Tours, Document and Record Reviews at the Eufaula Adolescent Center, Corrected Version, Marci White, April 25, 1995 (Redacted).
115. *Lynch v. Baxley,* 386 F.Supp 378 (December 14, 1974).
116. Author's Interview of Ashley, *Wyatt v. Poundstone,* 892 F.Supp 1410 (July 11, 1995).
117. *The Asheville Citizen-Times,* "Sex Scandal at Girls Prison Results in Firings, Lawsuit," June 18, 2001; *The Edwardsville Intelligencer,* "Lawsuit Swells Over Youth Center," October 1, 2002; *Iowa City Press-Citizen,* "Guards Fired in Girls-Prison Scandal, Lawsuit Alleges Teens Had Sex with Employees," June 18, 2001; *Southern Illinoisan,* "Sex Scandal at State-Run Girls Prison Results in Firings, Lawsuit," June 18, 2001; *The Birmingham News,* "CHALKVILLE: $12.5 Million Paid to End Sex Scandal at DYS," May 5, 2007.
118. *The Birmingham News,* "CHALKVILLE: $12.5 Million Paid to End Sex Scandal at DYS," May 5, 2007.

Chapter Twenty

119. Author's Interview of Russell James Cole, *Wyatt v. Poundstone,* 892 F.Supp 1410 (July 11, 1995).

120. *Stockton v. AL Industrial School for Negro Children,* Plaintiff's Complaint, January 21, 1969; *Stockton v. AL Industrial School for Negro Children,* Plaintiff's Complaint in Intervention, November 6, 1969.
121. *D.R. ex rel. Robinson v. Phyfer,* 906 F.Supp. 637 (December 6, 1995).
122. *Bozeman v. Orum,* 199 F.Supp. 2nd 1216 (2002); *Bozeman v. Orum,* 302 F.Supp. 2nd 1310 (2004); *Bozeman v. Orum,* 422 F.3rd 1265 (11th Cir. 2005).

Chapter Twenty-One

123. Author's Interview of Joshua, *Wyatt v. Poundstone,* 892 F.Supp 1410 (July 11, 1995).
124. "Institutional Policies on the Use of Physical Restraints on Children," Janice Selekman and Barbara Synder, *Pediatric Nursing,* Vol. 23, No. 5, September–October 1997.
125. "Minimizing the Need for Physical Restraint and Seclusion in Residential Youth Care Through Skill-Based Treatment Programming," Robert J. Jones and Gary D. Timbers, *Sage Journals,* Vol. 84, Issue 1, January 2003.
126. "Regulating Behavior Management Practices in Residential Treatment Facilities," Louise Murray and Gary Sefchik, *Children and Youth Services Review,* Vol. 14, No. 6, 1992, pp. 519–539.
127. "A Review of Crisis Intervention Training Programs for Schools," Michael Couvillon, Reece L. Peterson, Joseph B. Ryan, Brenda Scheuermann, Joanna Stegall, *TEACHING Exceptional Children,* Vol. 42, No. 5, 2010, pp. 6–17.
128. "The Use of Physical Restraint Interventions for Children and Adolescents in the Acute Care Setting," Committee on Pediatric Emergency Medicine, *American Academy of Pediatrics,* Vol. 99, No. 3, March 1997.
129. "Characteristics of Adolescents Frequently Restrained in Psychiatric Units in Norway: A Nationwide Study," Astrid Furre, Ragnhild Sorum Falk, Leiv Sadnvik, Svein Friis, Maria Knutsen, and Keitil Hanssen-Bauer, *Child and Adolescent Psychiatry and Mental Health,* January 12, 2017.
130. "Heavy-Tailed Distribution of Seclusion and Restraint Episodes in A State Psychiatric Hospital," Paul D. Whitehead, MD, Fredrik Liljeros, PhD, *Journal of the American Academy of Psychiatry and the Law,* Vol. 39, No. 1, 2011, pp. 93–99.

131. "Physical Restraint of Children and Adolescents in Mental Health Inpatient Services: A Systematic Review and Narrative Synthesis," Sim Nielson, Lucy Bray, Bernie Carter, and Joann Kiernan, *Journal of Child Health Care*, Vol. 25, No. 3, 2021, pp. 342–367.
132. "Patient Characteristics and Setting Variables Related to Use of Restraint on Four Inpatient Psychiatric Units for Youths," Kathleen R. Delaney, Louis Fogg, *Psychiatric Services*, Vol. 56, No. 2, February 2005, pp. 186–192.
133. "The Aggression-Coercion Cycle: Use of Seclusion and Restraint in a Child Psychiatric Hospital," Suzanne Goren, PhD, RN, Nirbhay N. Singh, PhD, Al M. Best, PhD, *Journal of Child and Family Studies*, Vol. 2, March 1993, pp. 61–73.
134. "Prevalence and Precursors of the use of Restraint and Seclusion in a Private Psychiatric Hospital: Comparison of Child and Adolescent Patients," David L. Pogge, Stephen Pappalardo, Martin Buccolo, Philip D. Harvey, *Administrative Policy Mental Health*, Vol. 40, 2013, pp. 224–231.
135. "Impact of a Mandatory Behavioral Consultation on Seclusion/ Restraint Utilization in a Psychiatric Hospital," Dennis C. Donat, Pergamon, *Journal of Behavior Therapy and Experimental Psychiatry*, Vol. 29, 1998, pp. 13–19.
136. "The Tradition of Toughness: A Study of Nonprofessional Nursing Care in Psychiatric Settings," Eileen Frances Morrison, RN, PhD, *IMAGE: Journal of Nursing Scholarship*, Vol. 22, No. 1, Spring 1990.
137. "Seclusion and Restraint of Children: A Literature Review," John Julian, BSN RN, *Journal of Child and Adolescent Psychiatric Nursing*, Vol. 13, No. 4, October–December 2000.

Chapter Twenty-Three

138. *Wyatt v. Stickney*, 344 F.Supp 373 (April 13, 1972).
139. United States Department of Justice, Civil Rights Division, United States Assistant Attorney General, United States Attorney in Montgomery, Amicus Curiae Trial Brief, (October 9, 1979).
140. *Dolihite v. Videon*, 847 F.Supp. 918, 923 (March 21, 1994).
141. *Wyatt by and Through Rawlins v. Rogers*, 985 F.Supp. 1356 (December 15, 1997); *Alabama Journal*, "James Asks to Direct Mental Health System," October 16, 1979; *Wyatt v. Ireland*, No. 3195-N, Federal District Court Order January 15, 1980.

142. Defendants' Trial Memorandum, *Wyatt v. Ireland,* No. 3195-N, October 15, 1979; *Wyatt v. Wallis,* No. 3195, 1986 WL 69194 (September 22, 1986).
143. Subject: Erwin Griswold Correspondence, Memorandum to Attorney General William French Smith, John Roberts Special Assistant to the Attorney General, December 11, 1981; Subject: Alabama Mental Case, Memorandum to Assistant Attorney General Civil Rights Division Wm. Bradford Reynolds and Special Assistant to the Assistant Attorney General, John Roberts Special Assistant to the Attorney General, December 11, 1981.

Chapter Twenty-Four

144. *From Courtroom to Clinic: Legal Cases that Changed Mental Health Treatment,* Peter Ash, Cambridge University Press, Copyright 2019, pp. 7–8.
145. *The Los Angeles Times,* "Alabama Hospital—A Concentration Camp," October 18, 1971; *Alabama Journal,* "Mental Care Backers Ask State to Halt Non-Essential Funds," September 1, 1971.

Chapter Twenty-Five

146. Twenty-Second Judicial Circuit Court of Alabama, Covington County, Public Criminal File of Wayne Alton Tatum, *State of Alabama v. Wayne Alton Tatum,* Case No. CC-2003-307, Author's Review, April 24, 2006.

Chapter Twenty-Six

147. *Dolihite v. Videon,* 847 F.Supp. 918 (March 21, 1994).
148. *Dolihite v. Maughon by and Through Videon,* 74 F.3d 1027 (January 23, 1996).
149. Author's Interview of Michael Dolihite, March 7, 2007.

Chapter Twenty-Seven

150. Author's Interview of Michael Dolihite, March 7, 2007.
151. *The Montgomery Advertiser,* "Allegations of Abuse Reveal Program That Seems to Work," February 2, 1986.
152. *Dolihite v. Videon,* 847 F.Supp. 918 (March 21, 1994).

153. *Birmingham Post-Herald*, "Opponents Say James Rewarding Supporters with Jobs," September 18, 1998; *The Selma Times-Journal*, "James Friends and Supporters Getting State Mental Health Jobs," September 18, 1998.
154. *Dolihite v. Maughon by and Through Videon*, 74 F.3d 1027 (January 23, 1996).
155. *The Montgomery Advertiser*, "State Settles with Family of Suicidal Teen," April 17, 1997.
156. *Weidinger v. Maughon*, 100 F.3rd 969, Depositions of Staff Members.

Chapter Twenty-Eight

157. *Wyatt v. Stickney*, 344 F.Supp 373, Appendix A Minimal Constitutional Standards for Adequate Treatment of the Mentally Ill (April 13, 1972).
158. *Wyatt v. Rogers*, 985 F.Supp. 1356 (M.D. Ala. 1997).
159. Evaluation of Tours, Document and Record Reviews at the Eufaula Adolescent Center, Corrected Version, Marci White, April 25, 1995 (Redacted).
160. Author's Interview of Wayne Alton Tatum, *Wyatt v. Poundstone*, 892 F.Supp 1410 (July 11, 1995).
161. Author's Interview of Wayne Alton Tatum, G. K. Fountain Correctional Facility (April 5, 2007).

Chapter Thirty

162. Evaluation of Tours, Document and Record Reviews at the Eufaula Adolescent Center, Corrected Version, Marci White, April 25, 1995 (Redacted).
163. *Wyatt v. Poundstone*, 892 F. Supp 1410 (July 11, 1995).

Chapter Thirty-Two

164. "Reflections on Frank M. Johnson," John Lewis, *The Yale Law Journal*, Vol. 209, Issue 6, April 2000, pp. 1253–1256.
165. *The Montgomery Advertiser*, "Frank Johnson: Doing The Right Thing," March 25, 1990.
166. The Academy of Achievement Interview, Judge Frank M. Johnson, Jr., Presidential Medal of Freedom, March 16, 1991.
167. *The New York Times*, "Frank M. Johnson Jr., Judge Whose Rulings Helped Desegregate the South, Dies at 80," July 24, 1999.

168. Testimony of Wayne Alton Tatum, *Wyatt v. Poundstone*, 892 F.Supp 1410 (July 11, 1995).
169. *Wyatt v. Poundstone*, 892 F.Supp 1410 (July 11, 1995).
170. Evaluation of Tours, Document and Record Reviews at the Eufaula Adolescent Center, Corrected Version, Marci White, April 25, 1995 (Redacted).

Chapter Thirty-Three

171. Testimony of Wayne Alton Tatum, *Wyatt v. Poundstone*, 892 F.Supp 1410 (July 11, 1995).

Chapter Thirty-Four

172. *Wyatt v. Poundstone*, 892 F.Supp 1410 (July 11, 1995).
173. Author's Interview of Michael Dolihite, March 7, 2007.
174. Letter to the Editor, Dr. Peter Bryce, *Medico-Legal Journal*, October 8, 1891.
175. Author's Interview of Wayne Alton Tatum, G. K. Fountain Correctional Facility (April 5, 2007).
176. *The Montgomery Advertiser*, "Changes Define Clark's Relationship with Black Leaders," March 24, 1994.
177. *Columbus Ledger-Enquirer*, "House Speaker's Home Town Spared Cuts," February 10, 1996; *Pensacola News Journal*, "Center with 12 Patients, 140 Workers Stays Open," February 10, 1996.
178. *Pensacola News Journal*, "Center with 12 Patients, 140 Workers Stays Open," February 10, 1996; *The Montgomery Advertiser*, "Adolescent Center May Be Closed," February 9, 1996; *The Montgomery Advertiser*, "Opinion, More Examples," February 16, 1996; *The Montgomery Advertiser*, "DYS Plans to Revamp Adolescent Facility," May 7, 1996.

Chapter Thirty-Five

179. *The Los Angeles Times*, "Qualified by Sad Experience, Head of Children's Legal Agency Has Been Through the Hardships of Neglect and Foster Care Firsthand," May 3, 1996.

Afterword

180. Los Angeles County Grand Jury Report 2001, pp. 205–275.

181. California Assembly Bill 2777, Chapter 442, Approved by the Governor, September 19, 2022.

182. *The Los Angeles Times,* "Decades Later, Former Foster Children Allege Abuse at MacLaren Children Center," May 17, 2022; *The Mercury News,* "Sex Abuse Victims Describe Horrors at Notorious California Foster Care Facility," June 10, 2022.

183. The Family First Prevention Services Act (H.R. 5456 [Family First]) was signed into law as part of the Bipartisan Budget Act on February 9, 2018, as Public Law 115-123.

184. Family First Implementation: A One-Year Review of State Progress in Reforming Congregate Care, American Academy of Pediatrics and Chapin Hall at the University of Chicago, March 2023.

185. *Best Practices for Residential Interventions for Youth and their Families, A Resource Guide for Judges and Legal Partners with Involvement in the Children's Dependency Court System,* Association of Children's Residential Centers, February 2017.

186. *Away From Home, Youth Experiences of Institutional Placements in Foster Care,* Sarah Fathallah and Sarah Sullivan, Think of Us, July 2021.

187. Letter to the Honorable Mitch McConnell, Majority Leader United States Senate and the Honorable Harry Reid, Minority Leader United States Senate, September 6, 2016.

188. "What Are the Outcomes for Youth Placed in Group and Institutional Settings?" Casey Family Programs, Updated June 2022.

189. "Five Facts About the Troubled Teen Industry," Cathy Krebs, American Bar Association, Children's Rights Litigation, Practice Points, October 21, 2021.

190. *The New Yorker,* "The Shadow Penal System for Struggling Kids," October 11, 2021; *The New York Times, Opinion,* "Can You Punish a Child's Mental Health Problems Away?" October 11, 2022.

191. *Helena Independent Record,* "Senator Looks to Redirect Regulatory Bill Over 'Troubled Teen Industry,'" March 27, 2023; *Sky News,* "Neglect and Abuse: Inside the US 'Troubled Teen' Industry," February 28, 2023; *Fox 4,* "CCHR Calls for Oversight of Troubled Teen Industry Due to Systemic Abuse," March 27, 2023; *NBC News,* "Board School Ignored Teen's Sickness Complaints Before She Died, Ex-staffers Say," January 26, 2023; *Baptist News Global,* Analysis, "The Troubled Teen Industry, Often Linked to Religion, Is Dangerous and Deadly," November 3, 2022; *The Fayetteville Observer,* "Locked Away

Investigation, Psychiatric Center Fail Many Children. North Carolina Keeps Spending Gobs of Money on Them," November 17, 2021; *The Washington Post,* Opinion, "America's 'Troubled Teen Industry' Needs Reform so Kids Can Avoid the Abuse I Endured," Paris Hilton, October 18, 2021; *The Salt Lake Tribune,* "Read the Violation Reports and Inspections for Utah's 'Troubled-Teen' Treatment Centers," March 4, 2021; *The Dallas Morning News,* "Chaos, Riots, Arrests of Children at Private Foster Treatment Facility Outrage Judge, State Leaders," February 9, 2021; *The Salt Lake Tribune,* "Provo Canyon School's History of Abuse Accusations Spans Decades, Far Beyond Paris Hilton," September 20, 2020; *The New York Times,* "Three Charged in Death of Michigan Teenager Restrained at Youth Academy," June 24, 2020.

Acknowledgments

This book was not written alone. I am indebted to many people, and these are only a few. First, I want to thank my brilliant editor and dearest friend Gretchen Young. She stood by my first book, *Hope's Boy,* and now this second book. Gretchen has always been there for me with her spot-on advice and boundless encouragement. She stands at the top of the publishing world, and having her at my side has been one of my greatest honors. From start to finish, Brenda Copeland was lovely to work with while editing the manuscript. She is one of the very best and also a friend. My thanks go to my delightful agents, Jennifer Unter and Jen Nadol, who spotted a book proposal and believed in the importance of the story that it had to tell.

I will forever admire the Bazelon Center for Mental Health Law, Ira Burnim, Claudia Schlosberg, Shelley Jackson, Ellen Harris, and Mary Giliberti. Their lifelong advocacy has brought inclusion, compassion, and justice to the lives of so many. James Tucker of the Alabama Disabilities Advocacy Program (ADAP) will forever be my hero. He hosted me during my trips back and forth to Alabama for my research and interviews. His diligent reading of the manuscript made it a better book, and I could not have written it without him. Marci White has spent her career pressing to improve the lives of adults and children with mental illness. I am deeply grateful for her thoughtful reviews of the manuscript and advice. Marci's expertise was invaluable to the fight for justice at Eufaula.

When Wayne Tatum testified at the trial, he was a young boy who dared to tell the truth about the Eufaula Adolescent Center when no adult would. Wayne made a difference that will last forever. I had the high honor of meeting Michael Dolihite, the father of David Dolihite. I sincerely thank Michael for sharing with me what happened to his son. The Dolihites are an extraordinary family, one filled with boundless love. Ricky Wyatt had me at his home. Brave and resilient, Ricky stepped forward as the lawsuit's named plaintiff. What are known as the "Wyatt Standards" laid the groundwork for the rights of people with mental illness and developmental disabilities in our country. They are named for him—deservedly so.

The Rockefeller Foundation and its Bellagio Center Residency Program graciously hosted me and gave me time to think and write. The staff at Alabama's Department of Archives and History gave me access to materials I would have never found on my own. The kind and patient clerks at the Frank M. Johnson Courthouse spent days locating decades of pleadings, evidence files, and hundreds of other documents that spanned across the history of the lawsuit.

Above all, I am thankful to my partner, Dr. Scott Young, who was always there to listen to an idea or read an addition to the manuscript—after an exhausting day of giving all he had for his patients at the Mayo Clinic. He is my greatest happiness, trust, and love. His sons, Bradford Young and Kyle Young, have brought joy and laughter to my life since the day I met them.

My admiration and respect will always remain for the individuals and families who struggle with mental illness, confront the injustice that comes with it, and rise above it every day. To the thousands of children who survived Los Angeles County's MacLaren Hall, I am honored to be one of you. And finally, my heart goes to my mom, Hope, and my grandma, Caroline—you forgave unfairness and hardship, and you loved me with all you had. The best of me belongs to you.